CIVIL RIGHTS STRUGGLES around the WORLD

YOU ARE *NOW* ON INDIAN LAND

THE AMERICAN INDIAN OCCUPATION

OF ALCATRAZ ISLAND

California, 1969

MARGARET J. **GOLDSTEIN**

 TFCB TWENTY-FIRST CENTURY BOOKS ■ MINNEAPOLIS

For Francie. This time I really mean it.

Cover photo: Indian occupiers moments after the removal from Alcatraz Island on June 11, 1971. They are (from left): Harold Patty, a Paiute from Nevada; Oohosis, a Cree from Canada; Peggy Lee Ellenwood, a Sioux from Wolf Point, Montana; Sandy Berger, from Fort Hall, Idaho.

Copyright © 2011 by Margaret J. Goldstein

Twenty-First Century Books
A division of Lerner Publishing Group, Inc.
241 First Avenue North
Minneapolis, MN 55401 U.S.A.

Website address: www.lernerbooks.com

Library of Congress Cataloging-in-Publication Data

Goldstein, Margaret J.
    You are now on Indian land: the American Indian occupation of Alcatraz Island, California, 1969 / by
Margaret J. Goldstein.
        p.   cm. — (Civil rights struggles around the world)
    Includes bibliographical references and index.
    ISBN 978-0-7613-5769-8 (lib. bdg. : alk. paper)
        1. Alcatraz Island (Calif.)—History—Indian occupation, 1969–1971—Juvenile literature. 2. Indians of
North America—Civil rights—History—20th century—Juvenile literature. 3. Indians of North America—
Land tenure—History—20th century—Juvenile literature. 4. Indians of North America—Politics and
government—20th century—Juvenile literature. I. Title.
E78.C15G58 2011
323.1197—dc22   2010005551

Manufactured in the United States of America
1 – CG – 12/31/10

CONTENTS

"THE INDIANS HAVE LANDED"

Nothing seemed out of the ordinary at the No Name Bar, a waterfront hangout in Sausalito, California. A few cops strolled in after midnight, as they often did, taking a quick look around for troublemakers. Bar manager Peter Bowen nodded politely. No problems here, he assured the officers. Thanks for checking. The cops left, and Bowen breathed a sigh of relief. It was nearing two in the morning, closing time at the No Name. Most of the remaining drinkers headed for home. But Bowen and a small group of bar patrons had another destination: Alcatraz Island in San Francisco Bay, about fifteen minutes away by boat.

Leaving his bartender to close up for the night, Bowen slipped out the back door with a half dozen others. Although the cops didn't know it, a larger group had gathered at a pier near the No Name. Many carried sleeping bags, backpacks, and other bundles. They moved quickly and quietly through the darkness. If the police were to spot them, their mission would be over before it had begun.

Bowen had arranged for three boats, including his own boat, *Seaweed*, to transport the group to Alcatraz. But the crowd was bigger than expected. It would take two trips to get everyone from Sausalito to the island. That made the voyage even riskier. The longer it took, the better the chances the Coast Guard would stop them, arrest everyone on board, and maybe even confiscate the boats. To escape detection, Bowen and the other skippers (boat operators) turned off the lights on their boats and headed for the 12-acre (4.8-hectare) island in darkness.

Alcatraz Island, nicknamed the Rock, is best known as the site of a former federal prison. For almost thirty years, from 1934 to 1963, it held some of the nation's most notorious criminals, including Al Capone and George "Machine Gun" Kelly. Prisoners sometimes attempted daring escapes from Alcatraz. But on this night, November 20, 1969, people were trying to sneak onto Alcatraz. They braved the strong currents and chilly waters of San Francisco Bay not to leave the Rock but to capture it.

Most of the passengers on board the three boats were American Indians, or Native Americans—mostly college students from Los Angeles, California, and the San Francisco Bay Area. Their mission was a bold one—to reclaim Alcatraz Island for Indian people and to establish an Indian cultural center and university on the island. Their mission was also a symbolic one. The takeover of Alcatraz would signal a new era of pride, power, and self-determination for the Native Americans of North America. "We came to Alcatraz with an idea," wrote Peter Blue Cloud, one of the occupiers and a member of the Mohawk tribe. "We would unite our people and show the world that the Indian spirit would live forever."

Cruising in the dark, the boats headed for the old prison dock on Alcatraz. One after another, the skippers pulled their boats alongside a water barge tied to the dock. Quickly, the passengers scrambled onto the barge, hauling boxes and bags of gear. After unloading, each skipper headed back to Sausalito to pick up another round of passengers.

The first group on the island found themselves in

This aerial view shows Alcatraz Island as it looked in 1963. In that year, the federal government shut down the prison on Alcatraz.

a strange and desolate landscape, filled with old rusty railings, broken-down machinery, and crumbling prison buildings. The island lighthouse sent a beam of light sweeping slowly across the horizon. Otherwise, Alcatraz was dark. But it was not completely deserted. Since the prison's closing in 1963, a small caretaker staff had lived on the island. That person guarded it from trespassers, tended the lighthouse and other machinery, and hosted the occasional government official from the mainland.

Security guard Glen Dodson was on duty that night in 1969. The students had made two previous attempts to occupy the island, so Dodson knew they might be coming. Sitting in his little guard shack near the dock, he thought he heard a boat engine. Then he saw hunched figures running through the darkness. He switched on a light near the dock and ran from the shack. "Mayday! Mayday!" he shouted to no one in particular. "The Indians have landed."

Caught in the act, the trespassers crouched in the shadows. But they had the advantage. There were dozens of them standing there, confronted by just one guard with no weapons. Most important, Dodson had left his guard shack without telephoning his superiors on the mainland. The authorities still didn't know about the landing.

Joe Bill, one of the student leaders, boldly stepped up to Dodson, smiled, and shook his hand. Dodson relaxed. He even told the invaders that he supported their cause—he was part Cherokee himself, he explained. Bill and several others accompanied Dodson back to the guard shack. They sat up with him for the rest of the night, joking and telling stories but mainly making sure that he didn't use the telephone.

By daybreak, after each boat had made two round-trips, ninety-two occupiers had come ashore on Alcatraz Island. As the sun rose, the newcomers explored the old prison buildings, including the cold and spooky main cell house. Some settled into more cozy residences, where the warden and other prison officers had once lived. Others lit bonfires, danced, and sang traditional Indian songs. Soon the invaders started to transform Alcatraz into their own territory. They hung a portrait of Apache chief Geronimo (1829–1909) above the fireplace in the warden's house. They painted graffiti on the old prison walls and road ramps. "You Are Now on Indian Land," declared one message. On the old prison water tower, the occupiers painted: "Welcome, Peace and Freedom . . . Home of the Free . . . Indian Land." One sign, posted earlier by the federal government, cautioned trespassers: "*Warning* Keep Off U.S. Property." The painters changed the sign to "*Warning* Keep Off Indian Property."

It didn't take long before the news of the invasion broke. Reporters working with the Indians soon alerted other members of the media. By the afternoon of November 20, word had reached the White House in Washington, D.C. An internal government bulletin flashed the news: "Indians Seize Alcatraz."

The takeover of Alcatraz Island had come off without a hitch. Soon much of the United States, and people around the world, would be focused on the island and its small band of occupiers. Their action had been a simple one—but what did it really mean for the United States and for American Indian people across North America?

Native Americans stand on Alcatraz Island on November 25, 1969. A sign above them declares Alcatraz to be Indian land.

CHAPTER 1

ANCESTORS

"There was a world before this one . . . the world of the first people, who were different from us altogether. Those people were very numerous, so numerous that if a count could be made of all the stars in the sky, all the feathers on birds, all the hairs and fur on animals, all the hairs on our own heads, they would not be so numerous as the first people."

—American Indian creation story, northern California

The Indian occupation of Alcatraz officially began on November 20, 1969. But the occupation had deep roots. The young people who took over Alcatraz wanted to create a better future for Native Americans in the United States. They also wanted recognition of and redress for (compensation) the many wrongs done to Native Americans over hundreds of years.

Native Americans were the original human inhabitants of the Western Hemisphere (North, Central, and South America and the surrounding waters). Their ancestors had migrated to the hemisphere from Asia, crossing a land bridge that once connected Siberia and Alaska around 13,000 B.C. or even earlier. For thousands of years, until Europeans began to explore and settle the Americas in the late 1400s, Native Americans were the only inhabitants.

It is impossible to generalize about the lives of Native Americans before European contact. Across the hemisphere, each tribe, or ethnic group, lived differently. Some tribes were farmers. Others lived by hunting animals or by fishing. Most tribes also gathered wild plants for food. Some Native American peoples lived in permanent villages or cities. Others traveled from place to place, following herds of game and other foods with the changing seasons.

The Ohlone people were a collection of tiny tribes living around the San Francisco Bay Area in California. They were just one of the hundreds of ethnic groups that inhabited North America before Europeans arrived. Like all Indian groups, the Ohlones had their unique customs. But examining the Ohlones can tell us a lot about Native American life as a whole.

PEOPLE OF THE COAST

In modern times, Alcatraz Island sits in the heart of one of the largest metropolitan areas in the United States. Modern visitors to the San Francisco Bay Area marvel at human-made wonders such as cable cars and the Golden Gate Bridge. The cities that surround the bay—San Francisco, Oakland, and their many suburbs—are crammed with millions of people, millions of cars, and millions of businesses. But on the edges of town, one can still get a glimpse of the natural splendors that filled the region many hundreds of years ago, when Ohlones were its only human inhabitants.

The Ohlones lived in a land of plenty. Thick forests of oak and redwood trees filled the San Francisco Bay Area. Grassy meadows were home to elk, deer, and antelope. Rivers running into the bay were filled with salmon and steelhead trout. Whales swam in the bay and along the Pacific coast. And vast flocks of ducks, gulls, and other birds filled the skies and the bay shore.

Nature provided the Ohlones with almost everything they needed. They made clothing and blankets from animal skins and furs. They made weapons and tools from stone, animal bones, horns, and shells. They wove baskets and fishing nets out of reeds, roots, willow shoots, and grasses. The Ohlone diet was varied. Nearby forests and meadows

American Indians canoe in the San Francisco Bay Area in this engraving from 1812 by Georg Heinrich.

provided acorns and other nuts, seeds, birds' eggs, fruits, berries, roots, mushrooms, and greens. The rivers, marshes, bay, and ocean provided vast stores of fish, mussels, oysters, clams, and other sea life. Using traps, slingshots, snares, and bows and arrows, Ohlone hunters killed ducks, seals, elks, rabbits, and just about any other animal that offered meat for their families and fellow villagers. Some valuables, such as glassy obsidian, which forms in fiery volcanoes, weren't found close to home. For these items, the Ohlones traded with people from other villages and other tribes.

The typical Ohlone village had about one hundred inhabitants— most related to one another by blood or marriage. People lived in dome-shaped houses made of a frame of willow tree poles with a covering of heavy grasses. These homes were temporary. The Ohlones moved with the seasons. In spring and summer, when food was plentiful, they lived in the hills surrounding the bay. During the rainy winter, they hunkered down on the shores of the bay, repairing tools and weapons and eating stocks of dried food they had saved up earlier in the year.

Ohlone life was guided by religion and rituals. Before hunting, men would spend many hours inside a sweat lodge. Sweating in the fierce heat prepared them physically and spiritually for the upcoming hunt. Birth, death, marriage, and children's coming of age were all accompanied by ceremonies, dances, songs, and special prayers. For the Ohlones, gods and spirits were everywhere—inside animals and plants, in rivers and forests, and in the moon and the stars. Certain locations were sacred.

Ohlone people put great stock in dreams. For instance, if a man dreamed about a mountain lion the night before a hunt, he felt blessed. He knew the lion would help make his hunt successful. Each extended family was headed by an animal-god, which gave family members special powers as well as responsibilities. When the animal-gods were pleased, people believed, they sent good fortune. But unhappy gods could send bad luck as well as illness.

Shamans, or medicine men and women, held a special status among the Ohlones. They could cure illness using herbs, barks, and roots, as well as magic. They could see the future and even influence the

The Ohlones built sweat lodges from saplings and brush. Inside such lodges, Ohlone men prepared themselves spiritually for hunting. This reconstructed sweat lodge is on display at the Coyote Hills Museum in California.

weather. But shamans could also work dark magic, and other Ohlones both respected and feared their powers.

The Ohlones had no writing system. They passed on information using stories, dances, and songs. Storytellers recited myths about the beginning of the world, when three animal-gods—Coyote, Eagle, and Hummingbird—created a new race of people.

Artwork was everywhere in Ohlone society. People typically wore strings of shell beads and feathered headdresses, with special costumes and ornaments for dances, hunting, and religious ceremonies. Ohlone baskets were made with intricately woven designs. Adults covered their bodies with tattoos. Much of Ohlone artwork was functional as well as decorative. When a girl reached puberty, for instance, older women tattooed her skin using black, blue, and green dyes. The markings told a potential husband what family the young woman belonged to and her family's animal-god, and therefore whether she was a suitable marriage partner.

The Ohlones had a strong sense of right and wrong. They relied on one another for survival. Everyone—from hunters who brought people food to women who wove baskets—knew his or her place in the social order. If someone did not follow the unwritten rules of Ohlone society, the other villagers might shun this person. Rule breakers also feared punishment from the gods. For these reasons, Ohlone society did not need a strong central government or a police force. Usually, one man served as chief of several villages. He was expected to be generous to the other villagers, especially those who were too old or too sick to care for themselves. But villagers also expected him to be careful not to squander precious resources. When the chief died, his eldest son usually inherited the job.

From generation to generation, the Ohlones lived like their ancestors had before them. Their lives were usually peaceful. They occasionally squabbled with neighboring groups, but warfare was not common. Unlike other Native Americans, who sometimes suffered from drought, famine, and brutal storms, the Ohlones enjoyed many comforts. The San Francisco Bay Area offered abundant food, mild weather, generous rainfall, and other natural riches. The Ohlones rarely went hungry.

They did not know much about the world beyond their winter and summer villages. They knew the ocean was to the west. The occasional trader brought goods or news from the east. But in 1492, when three European ships made landfall on the other side of the continent, the Ohlones had no way of knowing it.

"DISCOVERY"

In the fifteenth century, far from the peaceful and ritualistic world of the Ohlones, the nations of Europe were primed for change. In the big cities of Europe, people wondered what lay beyond the Atlantic Ocean. They reasoned that the world was round and that by sailing west across the Atlantic, they would reach Asia. They were right about that, but they didn't know that an entire hemisphere lay between Europe and Asia.

In 1492 Italian navigator Christopher Columbus, sailing on behalf of Spain, reached the Caribbean Sea, which sits between North and South America in the western Atlantic Ocean. Making landfall at several islands, Columbus thought he had reached the Indies, or East Asia, so he called the islanders Indians. That name stuck and came to refer to all original peoples of the Americas.

Columbus made four voyages to the Americas, all of them limited to the shores and islands of the Caribbean Sea. After Columbus, dozens of other European explorers crossed the Atlantic. Following long sea voyages, these sailors learned the extent of the Western Hemisphere, which stretches from the Arctic Ocean in the North to Cape Horn, the southernmost tip of South America. The explorers also saw the stores of riches that America had to offer: thick forests, mineral-filled mountains, inland lakes and rivers, and fur-bearing animals.

One by one, explorers claimed portions of the Americas on behalf of the nations that had sponsored their voyages. The Spanish claimed

In this 1754 illustration, explorer Christopher Columbus lands at San Salvador Island in the modern-day Bahamas on October 12, 1492.

vast regions of South and Central America. The French, the English, the Dutch, and other groups claimed parts of North America. In claiming lands, European nations asserted ownership by "right of discovery." In their view, the lands of the Western Hemisphere were an untouched and empty wilderness, available for the taking by the first European nation to "discover" them. This idea blatantly ignored the obvious: the lands were not untouched or uninhabited. They were home to the millions of Indian peoples whose ancestors had settled them thousands of years before. None of this mattered to the Europeans when they set out to explore and settle the Americas for themselves.

■ ■ ■ CONTACT

When white European sailors landed on their shores, Native Americans were at once curious, perplexed, frightened, and suspicious. They had never seen white people before nor had they seen the big sailing ships, horses, or iron weapons that the explorers brought to America. Some groups even thought the newcomers were gods. For their part, Europeans viewed Native Americans as "savages," since they lived close to nature and without the trappings of European civilization. One English chronicler described Virginia Indians as "so bad a people, having little of humanitie but shape, ignorant of Civilitie, of Arts . . . more brutish than the beasts they hunt, more wild and unmanly [than] that unmanned wild country, which they range rather than inhabite."

The Europeans came from a world heavily steeped in Christianity. Because the Native Americans practiced tribal religions, the Europeans called them heathens and pagans. These are derogatory names for people who do not recognize the Christian God.

Once Europeans had staked out territory, they set out to build forts and settlements and to exploit the riches of America. Since millions of Native Americans were already living on the lands they claimed, dealings with the American Indians were unavoidable.

Each European nation took a different approach to Indian relations. The French, who claimed portions of eastern Canada, the Great Lakes region, and later the Mississippi River valley, were mostly

This painting shows Native Americans peering through trees at European settlers in Virginia in the early 1600s. Indians were surprised and frightened to see white people for the first time. In Virginia, relations between the two groups soon turned tense.

interested in animal furs. French traders established friendly relations with Indian trappers and hunters, who supplied them with millions of furs. The furs—especially beaver furs, which were made into hats— sold at high prices in Europe. In exchange for furs, French traders gave European-made products to their Indian trading partners. These items included iron tools and kettles, brightly colored cloth, beads, firearms, and liquor.

The Spanish focused their efforts in South and Central America. They also explored and colonized (settled) parts of southern North America. The Spanish were more aggressive in their dealings with Indian people. They declared Native Americans to be subjects of the Spanish king and forced them to work at Spanish ranches, mines, forts, and missions (religious complexes). When tribes resisted, the result was often warfare. The Spanish had firearms and the Indians did not. As a result, battles were usually one-sided, with large numbers of Indian casualties compared to few Spanish ones.

The English and the Dutch, who settled along the Atlantic coast, took various approaches in their dealing with Native Americans. Sometimes they went to war to subdue hostile tribes. Sometimes they made alliances and traded with Indians. Sometimes they purchased their lands. The most famous early land purchase occurred in 1626. In that year, Peter Minuit, governor of the Dutch colony of New Netherland, bought Manhattan Island (site of modern-day New York City) from a group of Native Americans. The price was sixty guilders (about twenty-four dollars in modern times) worth of trade goods, including beads and cloth.

All the European powers tried to convert Native Americans from their "pagan" ways to the Christian faith. In English and French territories, various religious orders sent missionaries (religious teachers) to live among Native Americans and instruct them in Christian doctrine. The Spanish were very harsh in imposing Christianity on the Indian peoples they conquered. In early settlements in Texas and New Mexico, Spaniards forced Indians to convert to Christianity. Later, the Spanish built twenty-one missions in California. Using bribes, threats, and force, priests compelled California Indians to move to the missions. The mission Indians had to tend crops and animals, learn Spanish, practice Christianity, and abandon their traditional religions. The Spanish doled out harsh punishments to those who tried to escape.

Of all the early interactions between Europeans and Native Americans, the most destructive was disease. In Europe, smallpox, measles, scarlet fever, typhoid, cholera, and other diseases were widespread. Over many generations, Europeans had built up some immunity, or natural resistance, to these diseases. As a result, many Europeans survived disease outbreaks. When the Europeans arrived in the Americas, they brought diseases with them. But Native Americans had never encountered these diseases and had no resistance. Quickly, American Indians began to sicken and die. Smallpox was the worst—at times it wiped out whole villages and nearly whole tribes.

The Ohlones of what is now California encountered Europeans later than many other Native Americans. Although several Europeans sailed along the Pacific coast in the 1500s, they didn't explore inland or interact with Indian peoples. Contact didn't occur until 1769, when Spanish soldier Gaspar de Portolá led an expedition up the California coast to the San Francisco Bay. Three years later, Spaniard Juan Bautista de Anza led an expedition from New Mexico to central California. Anza established a fort that later became the city of San Francisco. Both expeditions encountered the Ohlone people.

Having never seen Europeans before, the Ohlones at first reacted to the Spanish with fear. Then they decided that the explorers were a new kind of animal-god, blessed with magical powers. In exchange for European-made beads and cloth, the Indians showered the newcomers with gifts.

After the initial Spanish expeditions, the missionaries arrived. They were determined to make California Indians into Christians and to make them live like Europeans. Between 1770 and 1797, the Spanish built six missions, or religious complexes, in Ohlone territory.

Priests (often accompanied by soldiers) pressured the Ohlones and their Indian neighbors to move to the missions. The mission-based Indians gave up their hunting-gathering lifestyles and instead learned European trades such as farming, ranching, blacksmithing, spinning, and weaving. Priests baptized the Indians and gave them instruction in Christian doctrine. The priests also forbade American Indian languages and religious practices. Some Indians continued to practice their traditional religions in secret.

For California Indians, life at the missions was not much different from slavery. Spanish soldiers made sure the Indians worked and prayed and did not try to run away. For those who defied the Spanish authorities, punishments were severe. Even worse, diseases such as smallpox and measles swept through the missions. Great numbers of Indian people died. Those who survived fell into despair. As new generations were born, fewer and fewer California Indians remembered the crafts, dances, languages, and rituals of their ancestors.

Mexico, which governed California between 1822 and 1848, shut down the missions in 1834. Most of the Ohlones and other California Indians took jobs on nearby farms and ranches. California became a U.S. territory in 1848 and a U.S. state in 1850. But the Ohlones and other California Indians were not granted U.S. citizenship. They had no rights or freedoms and suffered great discrimination at the hands of Anglo-American authorities.

In the San Francisco Bay Area, a few elder Ohlones tried to revive their old traditions, such as dances and deer hunting. But gradually the old-timers died out. Their offspring often intermarried with Spanish or Anglo Californians or with Indian people of other tribes. By the early twentieth century, Ohlone culture had nearly faded away.

But the 1960s brought a new awareness of Indian heritage and a struggle for Indian rights, including the takeover of Alcatraz. The takeover led to renewed interest in the people who had first lived around the San Francisco Bay. Since then modern Ohlone people have reclaimed their heritage, revived their culture, and asserted their identities as the original inhabitants of central California.

Native Americans grew sick from diseases passed on by Europeans. This painting depicts people of the Mandan nation dying of smallpox in 1837. Most of the Mandan people died in this epidemic. Smallpox and other diseases killed many other American Indian peoples.

LAND GRAB

The English, who controlled much of the Atlantic coast, were interested most of all in land. Starting in the early 1600s, hundreds of thousands of English settlers poured into North America, eager to create farms. But to do so, they had to clear the lands of the Native Americans who made their homes there.

A common vehicle for removing Indians from their traditional homelands was the land cession treaty. These treaties set forth terms of exchange: the Indians got goods and money, and the English got land. Treaties usually also established that English settlers would stick to one area, while Indians would stick to another. Treaties further said that as long as each group stayed in its own territory, both groups would keep the peace.

The English and other Europeans, used to buying and selling land and drawing up boundaries, were eager to sign treaties with Indians. But for Native Americans, land treaties were new. Native Americans had no concept of land ownership as it was understood by Europeans. They merely *used* land—hunting, fishing, or gathering wild plants there—without any notion of owning the land. Often, when Indians signed land cession treaties, they didn't realize they were signing away the right to ever use certain lands again.

Land cession treaties rarely held for long. Eventually, land-hungry settlers would trespass on lands that had been promised to American Indians. In other cases, the Indians, misunderstanding a treaty, would continue to hunt and gather plants on their traditional lands. After a treaty violation, peace usually crumbled. Indians attacked settlers, or settlers attacked Indians. Small hostile encounters soon turned into all-out warfare. The history of colonial America is marked by many wars between colonists and Native Americans: the Powhatan Wars in Virginia (1610–1614 and 1622–1632), and the Pequot War (1634–1638), and King Philip's War in New England (1675–1676), among others.

The colonists also had another war to wage. They fought for independence from Great Britain from 1775 to 1783. Many American Indian tribes allied themselves with the British during the fight. They hoped the British would better protect their rights. When Great Britain lost the war—and its American colonies—the Indians were on their own against the new U.S. government.

CHAPTER 2

CONQUEST

> We lived on our land as long as we can remember. No one knows how long ago we came there. . . . All of a sudden one white man came. We had no idea what for. This was the inspector. He came to our tribe with [Reverend] Mr. Himan. . . . They said the President told us to pack up—that we must move to the Indian Territory."
>
> —Standing Bear, Ponca tribe, circa 1878

The new United States was just as hungry for land as the old British colonies had been. As settlers moved farther west, they invariably encountered Native Americans. Settlers continued to sign treaties with Indians, but the arrangements were rarely fair. Often white agents pressured Indians to sign unfavorable treaties. And when treaties no longer suited them, whites often invalidated, altered, or simply ignored them. White authorities consistently punished Native Americans who violated treaties. But when white settlers did the same, the authorities rarely took action. So the American Indians sometimes acted in their own defense, attacking settlers. At this point, white governments would declare the Indians to be hostiles, or enemies, and send in militias (citizen military groups).

A series of small wars—Little Turtle's War, Tecumseh's Rebellion, the Black Hawk War, and others—raged in the Northwest Territories (the present-day Upper Midwest) in the late 1700s and early 1800s. In the Southeast, General (later U.S. president) Andrew Jackson led a number of successful campaigns against Indian tribes. With superior

Indian forces led by Tecumseh fought the U.S. Army at the Tippecanoe River in 1811. The Indians hoped to stop white European settlement of the upper Midwest.

arms and numbers, the white troops were most often victorious. When the battles were over, tribes were left with their warriors dead and their crops and villages destroyed. They sued for peace, ceded (gave up) more land to their opponents, and retreated farther into the wilderness.

The United States justified such wars by demonizing Native Americans. To white eyes, Indians were "savage bands of cruel marauders." Politicians stirred up fears of "wild Indians" capturing white women on the frontier and bloodthirsty warriors taking white scalps. All the while, politicians conveniently ignoring atrocities against Native Americans. To protect settlers, the U.S. military built forts and roads in the western wilderness. The forts and roads attracted traders and more settlers, who naturally wanted land of their own.

■ ■ ■ INDIAN TERRITORY

Hoping to resolve the "Indian problem" once and for all, the U.S. government took action. In 1825 it established a permanent "Indian Country" west of the Mississippi River. The borders stretched from the Red River in the South, north to the Missouri River. This chunk of land included much of present-day Oklahoma and about half of present-day Kansas and Nebraska.

In 1830 Congress passed the Indian Removal Act. This law authorized the relocation of Native American people to Indian Country, which became known as Indian Territory. The military began rounding up tribes from various regions and moving them to reservations (or parcels of land set aside for Indians) in Indian Territory. A government agency called the Bureau of Indian Affairs (BIA), part of the U.S. War Department, supervised Indians on the reservations. Uprooted and defeated, the unrelated tribes of Indian Territory mixed uneasily with one another. Unable to pursue their traditional hunting and gathering lifestyles, they came to rely more and more on the U.S. government for food and supplies. BIA agents assured Indians that "the Great White Father," or U.S. president, would treat them fairly if they played by his rules. Meanwhile, settlers streamed through Indian Country, clamoring for lands even farther west.

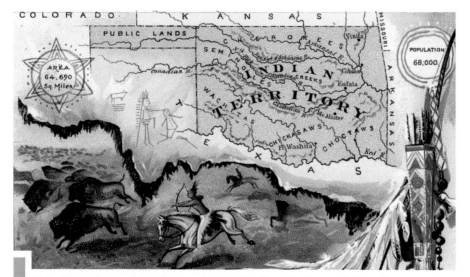

This 1890 illustration shows a map of Indian Territory. Originally set aside by the U.S. government in 1830, the land dwindled in size over the years (to less than half its original scope) as settlers claimed land there.

The U.S. government was especially eager to clear Native Americans from the southeastern United States. Settlers wanted this rich farmland for their own. The discovery of gold in northern Georgia in 1829 only heightened cries to open up the lands to settlement. Soldiers soon began rounding up southeastern tribes—the Choctaw, the Chickasaw, the Creek, and the Seminoles—and marching them northwest to Indian Territory.

The Cherokee inhabited a large territory in northern Georgia and Tennessee. By 1830 they had adopted some European ways. They formally protested removal to Indian Country through the U.S. legal system. The case went all the way to the Supreme Court—and the Cherokee won. But President Andrew Jackson, the famed "Indian fighter," ignored the Court's ruling. In the winter of 1838–1839, U.S. soldiers confined about fifteen thousand Cherokee people in stockades and then marched them to Indian Territory. The roundup and forced march were marked by brutality, hunger, disease, and death. About four thousand Cherokees died before or during the 800-mile (1,287-kilometer) trek. The Cherokee call it the Trail of Tears.

Although Congress had promised that Indian Territory would be a permanent home for Native Americans, that promise was soon broken. The railroads wanted portions of Indian Territory. Settlers wanted to farm the prairies of Kansas and Nebraska. The government soon began portioning off sections of Indian Territory for white settlement. By the mid-1850s, Indian Territory had been reduced to roughly the borders of present-day Oklahoma.

BUFFALO **SKINNERS**

Like all Native Americans, those of the Great Plains (a region of grassland between the Mississippi River in the east and the Rocky Mountains on the west) had a unique lifestyle. It depended greatly on the American bison, or buffalo, which lived in vast herds from Canada to Texas. Historians estimate that 75 million bison lived on the Great Plains in the mid-1800s. For the Plains Indians, the bison provided most of the necessities of life. Plains people made tepee coverings,

The famous western artist Charles Marion Russell painted this Native American bison hunt in 1887. Before the Spanish brought horses to the Americas in the 1500s, Indians hunted buffalo on foot.

"I WILL FIGHT NO MORE FOREVER"

The Indian Wars—against the American Indians—moved west across the Great Plains, into the Southwest, California, and the Pacific Northwest. For a time, the United States was preoccupied with its Civil War (1861–1865), so fighting Indians subsided. But after the war, battles for the West took on new vigor. By then the United States had acquired land all the way to the Pacific Ocean. Americans streamed into western

shields, and clothing out of bison hides. They made bowstrings from bison sinew and tools and weapons from bison bones. Bison meat gave them food. People burned bison dung as heating and cooking fuel.

Without the bison, Great Plains Indians could not survive. So when white hunters began shooting bison by the thousands, it spelled doom for the Indians of the Great Plains. The slaughter began in the 1840s and picked up speed when the railroad came across the Great Plains in the 1860s. White hunters came west with high-powered telescopic rifles. They slaughtered the herds for their meat and hides, which were shipped back east by rail. Some hunters killed bison simply for sport. Some U.S. officials encouraged bison hunting as a way to starve the Plains Indians and thus free up land for white settlement.

By the 1880s, the bison herds were nearly extinct (wiped out permanently). The American Indians who relied on the bison for survival grew increasingly desperate and many died of starvation.

territories to ranch, farm, mine, and open businesses. More than ever, the U.S. government wanted Native Americans out of the way.

The government sent the U.S. Cavalry (soldiers on horseback), staffed by many Civil War veterans, to carry out major campaigns against western tribes. "The only good Indians I ever saw were dead," declared General Philip Sheridan, a Civil War commander turned Indian fighter. Many Americans shared Sheridan's opinion.

More often than not, the Indian "wars" in the West were outright massacres. In Sand Creek in Colorado, a territorial militia attacked a peaceful Cheyenne encampment in 1864. The victims were mostly women and children. Other times, the fighting was more traditional, with Indian warriors of various tribes allied against the U.S. Cavalry.

The Sioux Wars of the late nineteenth century were some of the most fiercely fought battles for control of the West. Red Cloud's War of 1866 to 1868 is one example of many. This conflict took place in the Bighorn Mountains of southern Montana. There, the U.S. government had built the Bozeman Trail, which led from the east to Montana and Idaho goldfields. Gold-hungry miners followed the trail, which also took them through Sioux hunting grounds. In 1866 the Sioux warrior Red Cloud protested to U.S. authorities and demanded that the trail

In the 1860s, Red Cloud, a Sioux leader, demanded the U.S. government close the Bozeman Trail. The trail for settlers heading west crossed prime Sioux hunting grounds.

be closed. He noted that an earlier treaty had guaranteed that Sioux hunting lands would never be disturbed.

Disregarding the Sioux, the U.S. government built forts along the trail to protect miners. In retaliation, Sioux and Cheyenne fighters attacked the forts, as well as travelers on the trail. Red Cloud's War ended with the Treaty of Fort Laramie, also known as the Sioux Treaty of 1868. The treaty again guaranteed certain lands to the Sioux.

But still the settlers kept coming. Again looking for gold, they poured into the Black Hills of South Dakota and Wyoming, land that was sacred to the Sioux. Sioux leaders Crazy Horse and Sitting Bull were determined to resist them. In 1876, on the banks of the Little Bighorn River in southeastern Montana, a large force of Sioux, Cheyenne, and Arapaho fought a cavalry unit led by U.S. general George Custer. The battle is

COAST **TO COAST**

The United States acquired territory in vast chunks in the 1800s. With the Louisiana Purchase of 1803, the nation bought from France about 828,000 square miles (2.1 million sq. km) of land west of the Mississippi River. In 1845 the United States annexed (took over) Texas. Oregon Country came under U.S. control in 1846. Most of the Southwest became U.S. land in 1848, after war with Mexico. With each land acquisition, all the Amercian Indian peoples living there came under the rule of the U.S. government.

In acquiring land, Americans were guided by the concept of manifest destiny. This was the belief that it was God's will that the United States control North America between the Atlantic and Pacific oceans. The belief that God was on their side helped many white Americans accept the idea that the conquest of Native American peoples was their right.

The Indian Wars lasted from 1854 until 1890. Chief Joseph and the Nez Perce people of Idaho were among the last Indian peoples to battle the U.S. Army. The Nez Perce surrendered in 1877. This photo of Chief Joseph dates to 1899.

known as Custer's Last Stand, since he and most of his troops died in the battle. "They say we massacred him," Crazy Horse remarked, "but he would have done the same to us had we not defended ourselves and fought to the last."

Custer's Last Stand was pretty much the last stand for Native Americans in the West as well. Despite the victory at Little Bighorn, they could no longer hold off the U.S. Army. One by one, U.S. troops hunted down remaining Indian warriors. Soldiers then rounded up war-weary bands and moved them onto reservations across the West. After several victories, Chief Joseph finally surrendered his Nez Perce band to U.S. troops in 1877. He lamented:

I am tired of fighting. Our chiefs are killed. . . . The old men are all dead. . . .

My people, some of them, have run away to the hills, and have no blankets, no food; no one knows where they are— perhaps freezing to death.

I want to have time to look for my children and see how many I can find.

Maybe I shall find them among the dead.

Hear me, my chiefs. I am tired; my heart is sick and sad.
For where the sun now stands I will fight no more forever.

The last clash of the Indian Wars took place in 1890 at Wounded Knee Creek in South Dakota. It was yet another massacre, with more than two hundred Sioux men, women, and children killed by U.S. soldiers. American Indian resistance died almost completely after that. Native Americans had become a conquered people, mostly confined to reservations and living their lives at the mercy of the U.S. government.

Black Elk, a Sioux medicine man—a veteran of both the Battle of Little Bighorn and Wounded Knee—described the massacre at Wounded Knee many years afterward. "I did not know then how much was ended." He wrote,

When I look back now from this high hill of my old age, I can still see the butchered women and children lying heaped and scattered all along the crooked gulch as plain as when I saw them with eyes still young. And I can see that something else died there in the bloody mud, and was buried in the blizzard. A people's dream died there. It was a beautiful dream...the nation's hoop [united Indian community] is broken and scattered. There is no center any longer, and the sacred tree is dead.

CHAPTER 3

EXILES
IN THEIR OWN LAND

"Kill the Indian in him,
and save the man."

—Richard Pratt, founder of the Carlisle Indian
Industrial School in Pennsylvania, 1892

By the time the Indian Wars drew to a close, most Native Americans were confined to reservations. The BIA ran the reservations with absolute authority. The Indians there were considered wards of the United States. That is, the U.S. government acted as their guardians, much as parents are guardians of their children. By law Native Americans were not U.S. citizens. They had none of the rights of white male U.S. citizens and no say in their own governance. They could not leave the reservation without permission from BIA staff. Missionaries continued to school them in Christian doctrine. Indian religions and languages were forbidden.

Indian peoples were not only defeated but also heartbroken. Buffalo Bird Woman, a member of the Hidatsa tribe of North Dakota, looked back on the transition from freedom to reservation life:

> I am an old woman now. The buffaloes and black-tail deer are gone, and our Indian ways are almost gone. Sometimes I find it hard to believe that I ever lived them.
>
> My little son grew up in a white man's school. He can read books, and he owns cattle and has a farm. He is a leader among our Hidatsa people, helping teach them to follow the white man's road.
>
> He is kind to me. We no longer live in an earth lodge, but in a house with chimneys; and my son's wife cooks by a stove.
>
> But for me, I cannot forget our old ways.
>
> Often in summer I rise at daybreak and steal out to the cornfields; and as I hoe the corn I sing to it, as we did when I was young. No one cares for our corn songs now.
>
> Sometimes at evening I sit, looking out on the big Missouri [River]. The sun sets, and the dusk steals over the water. In the shadows I seem again to see our Indian village, with smoke curling upward from the earth lodges; and in the river's roar I hear the yells of the warriors, the laughter of little children as of old. It is but an old woman's dream. Again I see but shadows and hear only the roar of

the river; and tears come into my eyes. Our Indian life, I know, is gone forever.

■ ■ ■ ■ "THE EDUCATION OF THE RACE"

From the white point of view, the reservation system posed a number of problems. In the eyes of U.S. officials, Indian peoples were a "foreign" culture within U.S. boundaries. And their reservations—totaling about 138 million acres (56 million hectares)—in many cases encompassed prime farming, grazing, and mining lands. In the late 1800s, the U.S. government established two goals regarding Native Americans. First, it wanted to integrate (merge) Indian peoples into mainstream U.S. culture. Second, it wanted to free up more reservation lands for white settlement.

To achieve its first goal, the U.S. government established Indian schools. The plan was to take Native American children off the reservation and to educate them at boarding schools—operated by the government, church groups, or private organizations. Most boarding schools were located in cities far from the students' families and childhood homes.

In 1879 U.S. Army officer Richard H. Pratt founded the first government-funded Indian school, the Carlisle Indian Industrial School in Carlisle, Pennsylvania. Pratt believed there was nothing in Native American culture worth saving. "All the Indian there is in the race should be dead," Pratt declared. "Kill the Indian in him, and save the man."

To "kill the Indian," Pratt and other boarding school educators forbade any traces of Native American culture among students. School staff cut the hair of Indian boys, which was traditionally worn long; dressed boys and girls in European-style clothing; forbade them to speak Indian languages; and changed their Indian names to Anglo-American ones. "Only by complete isolation of the Indian child from his savage antecedents [background] can he be satisfactorily educated," wrote an Indian school superintendent in 1886.

In the following years, officials operated about one hundred Indian schools, mostly west of the Mississippi River. Often children had no choice but to attend. Police officers forcibly removed them from their homes if their families refused to send them to school.

At school the emphasis was heavy on discipline and physical punishment and light on academics. Most boys learned manual trades, such as carpentry and mechanics. Girls learned cooking and housekeeping. Educators believed that these were the job skills most suited to Indian

Native American children from the Apache tribe at the Carlisle Indian Industrial School in 1886. The school wanted students to adopt white culture. School staff would soon cut the boys' hair short and dress all the students in European-style clothing.

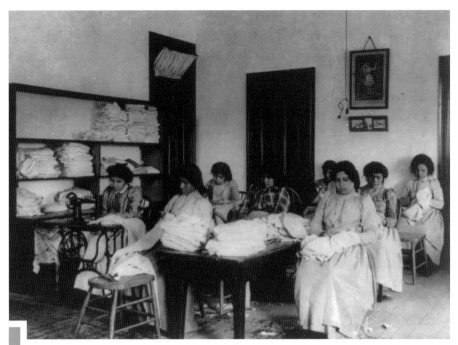

Indian girls learn how to use sewing machines to mend European-style clothing in 1901 at the Carlisle Indian Industrial School.

peoples. In summer months or for a year at a time, students lived in the nearby homes of white Christian families. Again, the idea was to train American Indian children in the ways of mainstream society. In most cases, host families treated the students as unpaid servants. In the worst cases, students endured physical abuse, harsh labor, and malnutrition at school and with host families.

FARMERS AND CITIZENS

Traditionally, most Native Americans had lived by hunting, fishing, and gathering wild plants—although some tribes, especially in the Southeast and Southwest, had grown corn and other crops. In the views of U.S. officials, if Indians were to be integrated into larger society, they had to make a living the way most other Americans did. In the late 1800s, that meant owning their own land and farming it.

In 1887 Congress passed the General Allotment Act, or Dawes Act.

Under this legislation (law), the government broke up some reservation lands into small parcels. It allotted (assigned) 160 acres (65 hectares) to each head of an Indian household and half that amount to single Indian men. After the allotments, the government sold any leftover lands to non-Indians. The Dawes Act did not give ownership of lands to Native Americans, however. The U.S. government still owned the allotted lands, which it held in trust for the Indian farmers. The law said that after twenty-five years, the Indian farmers would assume ownership.

The Dawes Act did not work out as planned. First, most American Indian peoples had no knowledge of or interest in farming. And many of the allotted lands had poor soil, unsuited to farming anyway. The U.S. government saw that Indians were not using the lands as it intended. So the government created new laws that allowed more non-Indians to purchase allotment lands. In the end, very few Native Americans took up farming. But a vast amount of reservation land—about 80 percent of the original 138 million acres (56 million hectares)—ended up under white control.

The final step in integrating Native Americans into U.S culture, the government thought, was to make them citizens of the United States. But the government didn't want to do that right away. In 1887 it determined that Indian people would need twenty-five years of wardship before they would be "competent" to take on the responsibilities of U.S. citizenship. Some Indian people won their citizenship ahead of schedule. For instance, the government granted citizenship to those who *did* take up farming under the Dawes Act and to those who served in the U.S. military. But the government was late to grant citizenship to the majority of Native Americans. It was not until 1924 that Congress passed the Indian Citizenship Act, finally granting citizenship rights to the continent's original inhabitants. Even so, a few states still denied Native Americans the right to vote.

NEW DEAL

In the early 1900s, Native Americans lived in limbo. Although the U.S. government had granted citizenship to Indians, it still treated them as wards. The BIA still took responsibility for their education, health care, and welfare. The government still shipped Indian children to boarding schools. What little American Indian culture remained was greatly eroded. Fewer and fewer people remembered the old Indian religions or languages. Many children who attended Indian schools headed for urban centers afterward, only occasionally returning to their reservation homes.

ALCATRAZ—**THE EARLY YEARS**

The American Indians of the San Francisco Bay Area had a long history with Alcatraz Island. For thousands of years, Indian peoples paddled to Alcatraz by canoe. They gathered birds' eggs from the island and netted sea animals along the shore. On long trips across the bay, the island served as a way station for travelers. Alcatraz is rocky and barren, with steep slopes and no natural cove or harbor for docking boats. Indian peoples never made permanent homes there. Some tribes thought the

Alcatraz was a federal prison when this photo was taken in 1940. Some of the nation's most notorious criminals—such as Al Capone and "Machine Gun" Kelly—were held there.

At the same time, a small kernel of American Indian activism was awakening. Indian people began to organize, creating the Society of American Indians in 1911 and the National Council of American Indians in 1926. Made up largely of Indians living and working in cities, both groups stressed that Indian peoples should take pride in their heritage and strive for success in mainstream U.S. society. Both groups also criticized the reservation system and the BIA.

island was cursed. They used it as a place of exile for those who broke the laws of their society. To other California Indians, the island was holy.

The first European to set foot on Alcatraz was probably Juan Manuel de Ayala, a Spanish military officer who arrived in 1775. Ayala named the island Isla de los Alcatrazes, or "Island of the Pelicans."

In the 1860s, the U.S. government set up an army prison on Alcatraz. The prison held not only soldiers who broke the law but also civilians, including many Native Americans. For instance, in 1895 the army locked up nineteen Hopi. These individuals had refused to abandon their traditional religion, as required by U.S. law, and had protested the removal of their children to Indian schools.

The military prison on Alcatraz operated until 1934. That year the facility became a federal penitentiary (prison), home for a time to mob leader Al Capone and other famous criminals. The government shut down the penitentiary in 1963.

Within the U.S. government, a few voices also called for reform. In 1928 the U.S. secretary of the interior requested a report on the state of Native American life. Called the Meriam Commission Report, this study came to some bleak conclusions. It found that most Indian peoples lived on reservations in abject poverty. Their education was poor, and their health care worse. They were demoralized (hopeless). The report said the BIA was doing a bad job and that the allotment system had been a failure.

Around this time, life became bleak for a majority of Americans—not just American Indians. The United States entered the Great Depression (1929–1942), a massive economic downturn. In response, President Franklin D. Roosevelt launched a program called the New Deal. It was designed to jump-start the economy, provide jobs to the unemployed, and improve social services for all Americans.

One piece of New Deal legislation was the Indian Reorganization Act, nicknamed the Indian New Deal. Its author was Commissioner of Indian Affairs John Collier. He was a longtime champion of American Indian rights and an admirer of American Indian cultures. Although not as far-reaching as Collier had hoped, the final law approved by Congress extended many new rights and benefits to Native Americans. The law strengthened tribal land rights. It allowed tribes to write constitutions and take on a degree of self-governance (although still with BIA oversight). It empowered tribes to set up businesses and encouraged the hiring of Indian people for BIA jobs. It also revamped tribal education—with an emphasis on reservation-based day schools instead of off-reservation boarding schools.

■ ■ ■ NO DEAL

Although promising, the Indian New Deal didn't bring significant change to Indian peoples. Congress never provided enough funds to carry out all the law's programs. And while the rest of the nation speeded ahead with new technology, such as hot and cold running water and electric power in homes, few reservations saw such improvements. What's more, many U.S. leaders still believed that Native Americans should be fully assimilated (merged) into mainstream U.S. society. They saw the Indian Reorganization Act, with its provisions for Indian-owned lands and businesses, as a barrier to this goal. In addition, some lawmakers wanted the federal government to be rid of its responsibilities to Native Americans altogether, including the costs of running the BIA.

In the 1940s, Congress devised a new approach to dealing with Native Americans. The idea was to terminate, or end, the special wardship relationship between Indian peoples and the federal government. In fact, the plan called for eliminating the wardship status of entire tribes—those tribes whose members were deemed ready for integration into white society. A new activist group, the National Congress of American Indians, organized to oppose the policy in 1944. But Congress moved forward with the plan. Termination officially began in 1953.

Supporters argued that the termination policy represented equality for Native Americans—since under termination they would become exactly like all other U.S. citizens. But for the one hundred-plus tribes that were terminated, the policy often meant disaster. Without the social, educational, and health-care services previously provided by the BIA, many American Indian peoples sank deeper into poverty. Many Indian-owned businesses foundered. Finally, termination freed up more reservation lands for sale to non-Indians. Thus, critics said, termination was just another land grab—a way for white people to buy up reservation land on the cheap.

Hand in hand with termination, the federal government instituted relocation. This program moved Native Americans off reservations and into eight designated cities. One of these cities was San Francisco. The relocation program was voluntary. More than one hundred thousand Indians—mostly young people—took the government up on its offer. Volunteers received a bus ticket to a big city. Once there, the government offered help in finding a job and a place to live. Once they found jobs, however—even just temporary ones—the relocated Indians were on their own. The government offered them no more assistance. It essentially abandoned the relocation volunteers in the big cities.

A third government policy of this era seemed more promising—at least at first. In 1946 Congress had created the Indian Claims Commission (ICC). Its job was to clear up old disputes about stolen tribal lands and broken treaties. The commission heard hundreds of cases that had sat pending for many years. It dismissed many of them as invalid. In other cases, the government paid cash awards to the tribes that brought the cases. But the system had one major flaw: payments were based on land values from the time the land had been taken. For instance, in 1959 the ICC awarded $29 million to the Indians of California. The money was compensation for 64 million acres (26 million hectares) of land stolen in 1853. The award amounted to 47 cents per acre (19 cents per hectare)—the value of the land in 1853. But of course, by 1959 this land was worth many thousands of times more. The ICC compensation system angered Native Americans. They did not want compensation based on one-hundred-year-old prices. They wanted fair compensation for stolen lands. In many cases, they wanted the land itself.

COWBOYS AND INDIANS

Until relocation, most non-Indian Americans had never met a Native American. Living far from remote reservations, most Americans got their ideas about Indians from popular culture—movies, books, and television. And the images presented by such media were almost always distorted, racist, and out-and-out fictitious. The typical American Indian of mid-twentieth-century pop culture was a wild warrior of the Great Plains. He wore a feathered headdress and terrorized virtuous white pioneers. This image was projected in countless "cowboy and Indian" movies, as well as television shows.

The Indians' nemesis (enemy) in these shows was generally a heroic white cavalry officer, sheriff, or cattle rancher, played most famously in this era by movie tough guy John Wayne. In *She Wore a Yellow Ribbon* (1949), for instance, Wayne plays cavalry captain Nathan Brittles. He and his valiant troopers must defeat a massive force of whooping, war-painted Indians on horseback, which of course they do. Almost never did the films or TV shows recount white atrocities against American Indian peoples. At best, the media showed Native Americans to be "noble savages"—doomed to destruction by the advance of superior white civilization.

In the twentieth century, the U.S. government encouraged Native Americans to leave reservations, and some did. The first to go were graduates of Indian schools. After receiving an Anglo-American-style education, many felt prepared for life and jobs in big U.S. cities. World War II (1939–1945) brought about the next migration. Many Native Americans moved to cities to take jobs in factories manufacturing war supplies. Approximately twenty-five thousand Native Americans served in the U.S. armed forces during World War II. In many cases, their wartime experience introduced them to urban life. Attracted by plentiful educational and job opportunities, many moved to cities after the war. The U.S. government's 1950s relocation program brought another wave of Indian peoples to big urban areas. In the following decades, more and more American Indians left for the cities. As they did, their ties to the reservation often weakened. In modern times, more than half of all Native Americans live off reservations.

Two Navajo Indians, serving with a U.S. Marine signal unit, operate a portable radio set during World War II in December 1943. The marines used a code based on the Navajo language to send secret messages.

John Wayne *(right)* plays a hero who fights off an Indian attack in *She Wore a Yellow Ribbon* (1949). The Indian is played by Chief John Big Tree. Through most of the twentieth century, Hollywood presented stereotypical views of Indian people.

The textbooks of the day also presented a lopsided view of history. From kindergarten to high school, U.S. schoolchildren learned how white pioneers had advanced steadily across North America, valiantly fighting the "savages" who stood in the way of progress. One textbook from 1960 described how Native Americans made "raids upon helpless frontier communities." The book did not mention that the Indians were usually protecting their territories from white settlers. An eighth-grade textbook from 1963 stated that the typical Native American "was cruel, and he dearly loved merciless war." A fifth-grade textbook, published in 1965, declared, "There were many Indian raids in the Ohio Valley [during the American Revolution of the 1700s]. . . . It was said that a woman could not safely go a hundred yards (91 meters) to milk a cow or a man to water his horse. Many cabins were burned and the families were massacred." Again and again, textbooks characterized American

Indians as the aggressors in U.S. history, not as people who were forced to fight to defend their own families, homes, and lands.

Even youngsters in Indian schools got a distorted view of their own history. Lucy Toledo, a Navajo, attended a California Indian school in the 1950s. She remembers, "Saturday night we had a movie. Do you know what the movie was about? Cowboys and Indians. Cowboys and Indians. Here we're getting all our people killed, and that's the kind of stuff they showed us."

By this time, Native Americans had had enough of such slander. They were appalled by the heartless policies of termination and relocation and were tired of politicians in Washington, D.C., deciding their fate. They were bitter over stolen tribal lands and broken treaties. They were ready once again to stand up and fight for their heritage, their culture, and their rights. And at this point, the rest of U.S. society was finally ready to listen.

CHAPTER 4

THE BIRTH OF INDIAN ACTIVISM

"The Hopi . . . have a prophecy that is at least 1,200 years old. It says that the People would be pushed off their land from the East to the West, and when they reached the Westernmost tip of America, they would begin to take back the land that was stolen from them."

—Richard Oakes, Mohawk, 1969 or 1970

As one of eight relocation centers, San Francisco had a large American Indian population in the early 1960s. As many as forty thousand Native Americans lived in the city and the surrounding Bay Area. Approximately two-thirds of them were relocation volunteers.

For those who were relocated, the transition from reservation to city life was often jarring. The U.S. government promised to help Indians find jobs, but this assistance was minimal. The poorly educated volunteers were usually qualified for only the lowest-paying jobs the city had to offer. The government also helped the volunteers find housing. But it often steered them to the dilapidated eastern edge of San Francisco's Mission District. Overwhelmed by urban life, some relocation volunteers returned to the reservation. But most remained and tried to make their way in unfamiliar surroundings.

The San Francisco Bay Area consists of nine counties that surround San Francisco. In the 1960s and early 1970s, many Native Americans lived there.

Native Americans eat together at the Intertribal Friendship House in Oakland, California, in 1972. This club brought many different Native American tribes together for socialization and discussion.

As the newcomers settled into the San Francisco Bay Area, people of the same tribe began to gravitate toward one another. They formed the Navaho Club, the Sioux Club, the Tlingit-Haida Club, and many others. The various clubs let people socialize and do business with others of the same background. People also used the clubs to maintain their native traditions. For instance, many clubs held regular gatherings called powwows, where people performed traditional rituals, music, and dances.

Some clubs and organizations, such as the Intertribal Friendship House in Oakland, were pantribal. At these clubs, people of different tribes began to reflect on problems of all urban Indians. They discussed the injustices endured by Native Americans as a whole—and what might be done to remedy them. Meanwhile, American Indian people in other big cities were doing the same.

■ BIGGER PICTURE

Native Americans weren't the only ones organizing for social justice at this time. Indian peoples in San Francisco and other cities took inspiration from the movement for African American civil rights. Using nonviolent tactics, civil rights activists protested against segregation (the forced separation of blacks and whites) in schools, restaurants, and other public places across the U.S. South. In defiance of segregation, African American college students held a series of "sit-ins" at whites-only lunch counters across the South. Other students campaigned for voting rights, which were frequently denied to African Americans in the South. African Americans and white supporters of all ages walked in protest marches and demonstrated in Washington, D.C., to call attention to racial injustice and to demand change.

Civil rights marchers enter Montgomery, Alabama, in 1965 during one of three marches in Alabama to demonstrate for voting rights. Martin Luther King, Jr., leader of the march, and his wife Coretta Scott King are in the center of the marchers.

Immediately after World War II, the United States started fighting the spread of Communism around the world. In theory, Communist governments grant equality to all citizens. All citizens share equally in the nation's wealth. In reality, many Communist governments are dictatorships that suppress all human rights and freedoms.

In the 1950s, Vietnamese Communists took control of North Vietnam, a nation in Southeast Asia, and they also wanted to take over South Vietnam. The United States sent troops to help South Vietnam fight the North Vietnamese. In eighteen years, the United States sent about 2.6 million troops to Vietnam. More than sixty thousand of these troops were Native Americans.

At home in the United States, many young people opposed the Vietnam War. They noted that in searching out Communist fighters, U.S. troops often maimed and killed innocent Vietnamese civilians, including women, children, and the elderly. U.S. troops also bombed, burned, and torched Vietnamese farms and villages,

African American activists got the most attention in the national media. But Native Americans did similar work in the late 1950s and early 1960s. In New York State in 1958, for instance, the state government planned to take over 1,383 acres (560 hectares) of Tuscarora land to build a reservoir (artificial lake). Tuscarora, Seneca, and Mohawk peoples

with no regard for the fate of the people who made their homes there. Many critics said that the United States should never have fought in Vietnam in the first place. They said the Vietnamese people should have been allowed to determine their own form of government, without interference from the United States.

Many minority troops, including African Americans and Native Americans, felt conflicted about fighting in Vietnam. The United States had a track record of oppression and abuse of poor, dark-skinned people at home. Now it was abusing and mistreating poor, dark-skinned people in Vietnam. Many Native American soldiers felt more of a kinship with the Vietnamese than they did with mainstream white Americans. "When I walk down the streets of Saigon [the capital of South Vietnam] those people look like my brothers and sisters," remarked Tuscarora antiwar activist Mad Bear Anderson, who visited Vietnam several times during the war."

protested the takeover using nonviolent tactics. They set up camp on the disputed land and challenged the authorities to remove them. The state backed down. One year later, Indian demonstrators gathered at BIA headquarters in Washington, D.C., to protest the termination of the wardship status of tribes.

In 1961 a group of young, college-educated Indians formed the National Indian Youth Council (NIYC). This group first took action in Washington State. There, American Indian peoples wanted access to certain river fishing areas. Their rights to these fisheries were guaranteed by federal treaties signed in 1854 and 1855, they pointed out. But state and local laws restricted fishing in these areas, and the authorities would not allow it. So, borrowing a tactic from civil rights activists, the NIYC staged a number of "fish-ins" in Washington— fishing the rivers in defiance of the law. The Indians also took their case to court. In 1963 the U.S. Court of Appeals upheld their fishing rights based on the old treaties.

■ ■ ■ THE ROAD TO ALCATRAZ

Adam Nordwall was a leader in the San Francisco Indian community in the early 1960s. A Minnesota-born Chippewa (known in the twenty-first century as the Ojibwa) and a graduate of two Indian schools, Nordwall had moved to San Francisco in 1950 to join family members. After landing a job at a pest control company, he decided to make the city his permanent home.

Nordwall's white coworkers didn't know any other Native Americans. They ridiculed him by calling him chief. They performed mock "war dances"—jumping around with fingers held above their heads like the feathers on an Indian headdress. Nordwall bore these offenses with good humor. He also did his best to blend into white society. By the mid-1950s, he was married with three children. The family moved to San Leandro, a Bay Area suburb.

As much as Nordwall managed to fit in, he was still an Indian and he was more and more drawn to the Bay Area Native American community. He attended powwows, joined the Intertribal Friendship House, and helped form the United Bay Area Council of American Indians. He became chairman of the council in 1962. At meetings with fellow Native Americans, Nordwall discussed termination, relocation, and the plight of both reservation and newly urban Indians.

He closely watched the growing civil rights movement—not only

Adam Nordwall sits with his wife and children in San Leandro, California, in 1961. *Left to right*: Julie, Adam, Adam Sr., Cheri, and Bobbie. Nordwall was a leader in the Bay Area Native American community.

to see how it could serve as a model for the Indian community but also how it was different. "All around us, and in the Bay Area especially, a social storm was rising over equal rights for those they called 'Negroes' then. . . . We watched from a quiet distance, aware of their frustration but separated from their aims. . . . It was our land that was being taken, our culture. We didn't want just an equal place in society. We wanted what was ours alone."

1964

By the early 1960s, the federal prison on Alcatraz Island was decrepit and needed expensive repairs. It was also more costly to keep prisoners

The last convicts at Alcatraz walk through the cell block in handcuffs on March 21, 1963. The prison was closed on that day.

on Alcatraz than to house them elsewhere. So in a cost-saving move, the U.S. government shut down the federal penitentiary on Alcatraz in 1963. The island and the prison building became surplus federal property. The government wasn't sure what to do with the island.

When the prison shut down, the Bay Area Indian community saw an opportunity to make a statement. Members of the Sioux Club of San Francisco had read about the Treaty of Fort Laramie, or Sioux Treaty of 1868, the agreement made after Red Cloud's War. Article 6 of this treaty is a lengthy and complicated passage. It discusses land "which is not mineral land, nor reserved by the United States for any special purposes other than Indian occupation." It states that American Indian men over the age of eighteen "shall be entitled to receive from the United States a patent" on rights to such land.

What did the passage mean exactly? Sioux Club member Belva Cottier took it to mean that any land that had been abandoned by the federal government would revert to the Sioux people. Thus the Sioux were entitled to Alcatraz, which the U.S. government no longer wanted.

Via the courts and the Indian Claims Commission, Native Americans were at that time fighting many legal battles to have their old treaty rights upheld. The Sioux Club was ready to put the Treaty of Fort Laramie to the test. Its members decided to stage a symbolic "invasion" of Alcatraz and also to pursue their claim in court.

"We did find a copy of the treaty," Cottier later recalled. "We turned it over to a lawyer who had six students research it as a legal document for about six weeks. . . . We looked up all the history and found out that many Indians had been held prisoners there [on Alcatraz], so in a way it already was Indian land. We studied the tides, planned strategy and looked for someone to take us to the Island."

The Sioux Club hired a tugboat and alerted the media. Then, on the afternoon of March 8, 1964, about forty American Indians took the short boat ride from Pier 41 in San Francisco to "invade" Alcatraz. Adding drama to the action, some of the invaders dressed in traditional Indian dance outfits, moccasins, and feathered headdresses. Adam Nordwall was part of the invading group, as was Belva Cottier and her husband, Allen. Elliot Leighton, a San Francisco attorney hired by the

Indians protest on Alcatraz on March 8, 1964, after "invading" the island to claim the land. They wore traditional outfits as a show of cultural pride.

Sioux Club, accompanied the invaders. About ten members of the press showed up as well.

When the boats unloaded, acting prison warden A. L. Aylworth confronted the Indian leaders. They were trespassing on federal property, he told them, and should leave immediately. At that point, Leighton came forward and read from a sheaf of papers, quoting the Sioux Treaty of 1868 and stating the Sioux's legal claim to the island.

Allen Cottier also read a formal statement: "Under the U.S. Code we as Sioux Indians are settling on Federal land no longer appropriated [used]."

With that, the invaders began a victory dance. Sioux Club member Walter Means and his son Russell hammered an old mop handle into the ground as a claim marker. Another club member flashed a mirror signal to the mainland: three glints for victory. Other Indians set up a green camp tent that was meant to stand in as a tepee.

By then Aylworth had called his boss, who caught a quick boat to the island. He too told the invaders to leave, and on the advice of Leighton, they did. The next day, the *San Francisco Examiner* reported on the "Wacky Indian Raid."

Few people took the invasion seriously. But attorney Leighton proceeded to file suit in district court, seeking title to Alcatraz on behalf of Richard McKenzie, one of the Sioux Club leaders. The government didn't take the case seriously either. Government attorneys said that Leighton and McKenzie were merely seeking publicity for the cause of Native Americans and that the Sioux didn't have a valid claim to Alcatraz. The court agreed and dismissed the case.

■ ■ ■ THE NEXT GENERATION

The civil rights movement kicked off an era of turbulence in the United States. On the heels of civil rights demonstrations, college students began protesting against U.S. involvement in the Vietnam War (1957– 1975). Soon many young people became more and more defiant. They questioned everything about their parents' lives. They rejected the "establishment" and the American dream of a traditional family life, a nine-to-five job, and a home in the suburbs. They questioned the U.S. government, the U.S. military, and other forms of authority. Inspired by the British rock band the Beatles, young men began to grow their hair long. Some refused to fight in the Vietnam War. Soon young people were exploring all sorts of new ideas: drug use, sexual freedom, Eastern religions, and environmentalism. They created the hippie movement, or counterculture. Its center was San Francisco.

Young people participate in an antiwar rally in front of San Francisco City Hall in 1968. The 1960s was a time of social upheaval and demand for change in the United States.

As the 1960s wore on, the rebellion continued to grow. African Americans became more defiant in their quest for equality. They spoke about black power. Some even talked of revolution—or overthrowing the government. Women, who were expected to be subservient to their husbands in this era, began to demand equality with men at home, in education, and in the workplace. They started a movement for women's lib—or liberation. Other oppressed minorities, including gays and Hispanics, also protested for equal rights.

■ ■ ■ RED POWER

The time had come for Native Americans to stand up and fight as well. In the Bay Area and other locales, Indians continued to gather at powwows and tribal events. They met for national conferences and lobbied politicians in Washington, D.C.

Across the United States, Native Americans continued to fight for treaty rights and sought compensation for stolen tribal lands. They also wanted to set the record straight about the history of Indian–white relations. They wanted to teach young people the truth about the Trail of Tears, massacres of Indian people, broken treaties, and other injustices. They criticized cowboy and Indian movies and textbooks that described Native Americans as "Bold, Flamboyant Savages of the Western Plains."

POVERTY IN INDIAN COUNTRY

On both reservations and in cities, most American Indian peoples lived in extreme poverty in the 1960s. Consider these statistics:

- Unemployment among Native Americans was 40 percent—ten times the national average.
- The average American Indian family's income was $1,500, one-fourth the national average.
- About 80 percent of reservation Indians lived below the poverty line.
- Life expectancy for Native Americans was forty-four years, twenty years less than the national average.
- American Indian infant mortality (death) rates were double the national average.
- School dropout rates for American Indians were twice the national average.
- Suicide rates for Indians were twice the national average.

Much 1960s activism was centered at universities, and Indian activism was no different. In the Bay Area, professors and students at San Francisco State (SFS) College, the University of California–Berkeley (UC–Berkeley), and the University of California–Los Angeles (UCLA) pressed school administrators to create Native American studies departments. They wanted scholars to be able to explore, shatter the myths about, and reveal the realities of Native American society and history.

> "Starting in 1967 at the University of New Mexico Law School, we read treaties, Indian legal history. It was just astonishing how unfair it was, how wrong it was. It [Alcatraz] was the kind of thing we needed."
>
> —John Echohawk, *Pawnee*, 1993

LaNada Boyer, a relocation volunteer from the Bannock Shoshone Fort Hall Reservation in Idaho, arrived at UC–Berkeley in 1968. Angry about the racism she had endured both in Indian schools and in her Idaho hometown, about the false promises of relocation, and about the mistreatment of American Indian people in general, she was quickly caught up in Indian activism on campus. In 1968 Boyer and Berkeley graduate student Lehman Brightman formed a student association called United Native Americans (UNA). Much more militant than earlier Bay Area Indian groups, UNA was determined to take American Indian activism to a new, more defiant level.

Whites had long before labeled Indians "red men," for a supposed red cast to their skin. Taking off on the notion of black power, Indian students were ready to take a stand for "red power." In its newspaper, *Warpath*, UNA announced:

The "Stoic, Silent Redman" of the past who turned the other cheek to white injustice is dead. (He died of frustration and heartbreak.) And in his place is an angry group of Indians who dare to speak up and voice their dissatisfaction at the world around them. Hate and despair have taken their toll and only action can quiet this smoldering anger that has fused this new Indian movement into being.

■ THIRD WORLD STRIKES

Twenty-six-year-old Mohawk Richard Oakes arrived in San Francisco from New York state also around 1968. He took a job tending bar; enrolled at SFS; and met and married Anne Marufo, a Pomo, who had five children from a previous marriage. Like LaNada Boyer, Oakes was attracted to Indian activism on campus. He joined the SFS Native American Studies group, discussed Indian history and politics with his fellow students and instructors, and learned all he could about the history of U.S. injustice to Native Americans.

San Francisco State—like many of the nation's colleges and universities—was seething with political activism at this time. SFS students protested against the draft (the legal selection of young men to serve in the military) and the Vietnam War—but they had other grievances as well. Black students thought the college should work harder to recruit and enroll minority members. They also wanted the college to create courses to examine African American history and culture, as well as the history of injustices endured by African Americans. Native American and Hispanic students had similar concerns regarding the college and their own history and culture.

In November 1968, the college fired George Murray. Murray was a graduate student instructor and also a member of the Black Panthers, an Oakland-based African American group that advocated violent overthrow of the U.S. government. The firing provided the spark that lit a fire on campus. The school's Black Students Union joined forces with the Third World Liberation Front, an activist group made up of

Demonstrators scale a wall at the administration building at San Francisco State College on December 6, 1967. The students demanded higher minority enrollment and minority studies programs at the college.

black, Hispanic, Asian, and Native American students. The coalition declared a "Third World Strike." It intended to shut down the college until the administration agreed to a set of fifteen demands to make the school and its curriculum more inclusive.

The minority students and their supporters gathered in great numbers around campus buildings, chanting, "On strike! Shut it down!"[30] It was impossible for classes to continue. The college called in the San Francisco police, who beat protesters with batons and arrested them by the hundreds. The strike dragged on for almost five months. After a series of negotiations, the college agreed to establish the Black Studies Department and School of Ethnic Studies, including courses in Native American studies.

Richard Oakes took part in the Third World Strike at SFS, although not in a leadership role. But the strike convinced him that the time had come to take more dramatic action on behalf of American Indian people.

AIM

Minneapolis, Minnesota, was a hotbed of American Indian activism in the late 1960s. Although not a relocation city, Minneapolis had a large Native American population. Like urban Native Americans elsewhere, these Indians mostly lived in poverty. The city police were particularly hostile and abusive to American Indian residents. Fed up with this treatment, Minneapolis Indians Dennis Banks, Clyde Bellecourt, and others decided to make a stand for change. They formed the American Indian Movement (AIM) in 1968. The group modeled itself loosely on the revolutionary black power group the Black Panthers. AIM spoke out against police brutality in Minneapolis and created programs to provide jobs, housing, and education to Minneapolis Indians. Within a few years, AIM chapters had opened in other cities. The group became increasingly militant and even determined to use violence, if necessary, to advance the cause of social justice for Native Americans. Since that time, Bellecourt still continues to direct AIM activities. Bank raises funds for a college in northern Minnesota serving mostly Native American students.

Meanwhile, across the bay in Berkeley, students launched a similar Third World Strike in January 1969. First, police came in to arrest the strikers and to break up the demonstrations with tear gas. When that failed to stop the strike, California governor Ronald Reagan sent in the

Students went on strike at UC–Berkeley in 1969. They struck to force the university to add African American and Native American studies programs. When police moved in to enforce order, students then protested against the cops. They held banners urging the "pigs" (police) to stay away.

National Guard. By the time the strike ended in March, 150 students had been arrested and 36 suspended from school. LaNada Boyer was arrested for assaulting a police officer, but the charges were later dropped. The university suspended her for one semester. Despite such punishments, the students were pleased with the final result of the strike: creation of the Department of Ethnic Studies at Berkeley.

CHAPTER 5

LANDING
PARTY

It would be fitting and symbolic that ships from all over the world, entering the Golden Gate [the San Francisco Bay] would first see Indian land, and thus be reminded of the true history of this nation. This tiny island would be a symbol of the great lands once ruled by free and noble Indians."

—Indians of All Tribes proclamation, November 1969

By 1969, six years after closing the federal prison at Alcatraz, the U.S. government still hadn't decided what to do with it. Should it turn the island into a museum? A park? The government entertained many different ideas. Finally, it decided to let San Francisco city officials make the call.

The 1964 invasion of Alcatraz hadn't made a lasting impression among Bay Area residents as a whole. But the area's Native Americans remembered it. Invader Adam Nordwall and others still hoped that Alcatraz could become Indian land in some form or another. In the summer of 1969, the Bay Area Council drew up a proposal to submit to the San Francisco Board of Supervisors. The plan called for the development of an American Indian spiritual center, an ecology center, a museum, and a school on Alcatraz Island.

The city had its own ideas for Alcatraz. It tentatively approved a proposal from Texas billionaire Lamar Hunt to fill the island with hotels, restaurants, casinos, and a space exploration museum. But many San Franciscans protested this plan. They thought Hunt's proposal was garish and that the island should serve an educational or cultural purpose, not a commercial one. In the face of protests, city officials cooled on Hunt's plan.

YOUNG BLOOD

The Bay Area Council was the established, mainstream American Indian advocacy group in San Francisco. Most of its members, such as Chairman Adam Nordwall, were middle-aged, with steady jobs, homes, and families. By contrast, the students enrolled in the new ethnic studies departments at UC–Berkeley and SFS were bold and brash. They were part of the new youth counterculture and less attached to social conventions.

The different groups didn't always agree on the best way to proceed with the fight for Indian rights. The Bay Area Council tried to work through accepted political channels. The students favored more dramatic protests. But the two factions (groups) had one thing in common: both had been considering the idea of Indians returning to Alcatraz.

When the San Francisco American Indian Center, on Valencia Street, burned down in mid-October 1969, that idea took on a new urgency. The Indian Center was a lifeline for Indians in the Bay Area. It offered assistance with employment, housing, health care, and legal problems. It also served as an important gathering and meeting place for Native American activists. After the fire, the entire American Indian community—from the Bay Area Council to the down-and-out residents of the eastern Mission District—felt the loss greatly.

At that time, Adam Nordwall got together with SFS student Richard Oakes. They spoke with Belva Cottier, initiator of the 1964 invasion, and drew up a plan for Indians to invade Alcatraz again—and this time to remain there. They planned to transform the island into a new Indian Center.

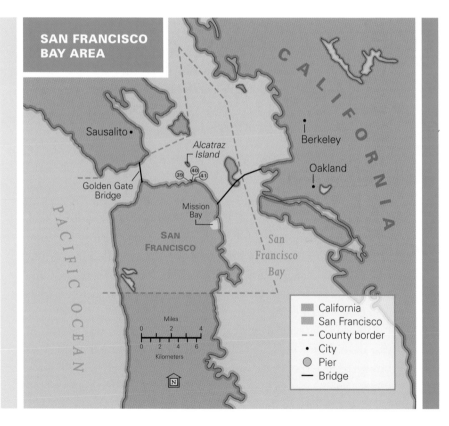

■ ■ ■ "TO THE GREAT WHITE FATHER"

The 1964 invasion of Alcatraz had been largely made by Sioux people. But the 1969 planners came from all different tribes. They wanted to claim Alcatraz on behalf of all Native American people, so they chose the name Indians of All Tribes for their invasion force. They drew up plans and alerted the media. Nordwall hired five charter boats to meet the invaders at Pier 39 on the morning of November 9.

On that morning, about seventy-five Native Americans were there. To declare their cultural pride, Nordwall and others were dressed in tribal outfits: fringed shawls, buckskin suits, beads, feathers, and headdresses. The press was there—but the boats did not show. Apparently, the skippers realized they could get in big trouble for assisting an illegal occupation of government land. They backed out without a word.

Nordwall panicked. The press was expecting a dramatic show—but there could be no invasion without boats. Stalling for time, Nordwall told Richard Oakes to read a proclamation that the organizers had prepared for the event. As TV cameras rolled and reporters scribbled, Oakes read a statement dripping with cynicism, sarcasm, and historic references:

> To the Great White Father and All His People:
>
> We, the native Americans, re-claim the land known as Alcatraz Island in the name of all American Indians by right of discovery. We wish to be fair and honorable in our dealings with the Caucasian [white] inhabitants of this land, and hereby offer the following treaty: We will purchase said Alcatraz Island for 24 dollars...in glass beads and red cloth, a precedent set by the white man's purchase of a similar island about 300 years ago. We know that $24 in trade goods...is more than was paid when Manhattan Island [New York City] was sold, but we offer that land values have risen over the years. Our offer of $1.24 per acre [50 cents per hectare] is greater than the 47 cents per acre [19 cents per hectare] the white men are now paying the California Indians for their land. We will give the inhabitants of this land a portion

of that land for their own, to be held in trust by the American Indian Government—for as long as the sun shall rise and rivers go down to the sea—to be administered by the Bureau of Caucasian Affairs....We will further guide the inhabitants in the proper way of living. We will offer them our religion, our education, our life-ways, in order to help them achieve our level of civilization and thus raise them and all their white brothers up from their savage and unhappy state. We offer this treaty in good faith and wish to be fair and honorable in our dealings with the white men.

The statement continued:

We feel that this so-called Alcatraz Island is more than suitable as an Indian reservation, as determined by the white man's own standards. By this we mean that this place resembles most Indian reservations, in that:

1. It is isolated from modern facilities, and without adequate means of transportation.
2. It has no fresh running water.
3. The sanitation facilities are inadequate.
4. There are no oil or mineral rights.
5. There is no industry and so unemployment is very great.
6. There are no health care facilities.
7. The soil is rocky and non-productive and the land does not support game.
8. There are no educational facilities.
9. The population has always been held as prisoners and kept dependent on others.

Further, it would be fitting and symbolic that ships from all over the world, entering the Golden Gate [the strait leading into San Francisco Bay], would first see Indian land, and thus be reminded of the true history of this nation. This tiny island would be a symbol of the great lands once ruled by free and noble Indians.

When Oakes had finished reading, some of the Indians began drumming, singing, and dancing. Meanwhile, Adam Nordwall improvised. On the pier, he approached a man named Ronald Craig, skipper of the ship *Monte Cristo*. Would Craig run some passengers out to Alcatraz? Nordwall asked. Craig agreed but said that he'd only circle

> **"The landing on Alcatraz Island is a symbol of our cultural right to land and to life. How are we to be charged with trespassing on the white man's land when the white man has taken all this land from us?"**
>
> —Indians of All Tribes, *press release, November 10, 1969*

the island a few times—he wouldn't land there. He also limited the trip to fifty passengers.

A symbolic boat trip was better than nothing, so fifty Native Americans boarded the *Monte Cristo* and set off for the island. On the roof of the captain's quarters, several passengers banged on a drum and sang Indian war songs. Members of the press followed the *Monte Cristo* in boats of their own.

On board the *Monte Cristo*, Richard Oakes was disappointed that there would be no Alcatraz landing. He was sick of symbolism—he wanted to really take over the island. So when the *Monte Cristo* got within a few hundred yards of Alcatraz, Oakes took off his shirt, jumped in the water, and started to swim. The other passengers cheered. Quickly, four other young men followed Oakes into the bay. The current was strong, and Oakes was swept off course. Eventually, though, all the swimmers reached the island safely. But there was no occupation that day. The Coast Guard soon arrived to ferry the invaders back to the mainland.

ANOTHER TRY

On the way back to Pier 39, the passengers aboard the *Monte Cristo* were fired up. "Do you want to go back and take Alcatraz?" Nordwall shouted. "Really take it?" The other passengers really did. So Nordwall arranged for another boat, *New Vera II*, to sneak back to Alcatraz that night.

The skipper charged Nordwall three dollars a head to take about twenty-five American Indians back to the island. But Nordwall neglected to tell the skipper that the group intended to disembark (get off the boat) when they got there. When *New Vera II* pulled up to the Alcatraz dock, students began to scramble off—much to the skipper's surprise. He realized then that he was party to an illegal takeover of government property—a role that could land him in big trouble. So before everyone had a chance to disembark, the skipper pulled away from the dock. Nevertheless, fourteen occupiers had made it safely onto the island.

The new landing party, which included

After surrendering to the U.S. Coast Guard, fourteen occupiers leave Alcatraz on the morning of November 10, 1969. Ten days later, more American Indian activists arrived to occupy the area.

Richard Oakes and LaNada Boyer, spent the night on Alcatraz, playing a game of hide-and-seek with the authorities who had arrived to apprehend them. In the morning, the Coast Guard told the invaders that no one would be arrested if they gave themselves up. Believing that a successful occupation needed more people and more planning, Oakes

> "There was the prison, with its catwalks [suspended walkways] and huge walls topped with coiled barbed wire. The old guard towers, now silent and empty, stood as grim sentinels [guardians] of the island's famous and horrific past."
>
> —Adam Nordwall, describing his first view of Alcatraz, 1969

surrendered the whole group. The Indians of All Tribes then released a defiant statement to the press. It read in part:

Our people have suffered at the hands of the white man ever since we welcomed the Pilgrims to our shores. In return for our help and kindness, the white man has stolen our lands, killed our people and decimated our way of life. We have been under the Bureau of Indian Affairs for over one hundred years, and as a result we have the highest rates of unemployment, of illness, of poverty—of all the sickness of modern life.

Now our young people cry out for social justice and for an opportunity to reclaim their proud heritage. The landing on Alcatraz Island is a symbol of our cultural right to land and to life. How are we to be charged with trespassing on the white man's land when the white man has taken all of this land from us?

■ ■ ■ AND ANOTHER

LaNada Boyer was upset that Oakes had surrendered the group to the Coast Guard. She had desperately wanted to remain on Alcatraz. Other student activists were equally determined to permanently occupy the island and planned a new invasion for November 20. Oakes drove all the way down to Los Angeles to recruit additional occupiers from the Indian Studies Department at UCLA.

The November 20 invasion force departed from the pier behind the No Name Bar in Sausalito, this time successfully landing more than ninety people on Alcatraz. Boyer was among these occupiers. She even brought her two-year-old son to the island. Richard Oakes was there too, as was his twelve-year-old stepdaughter, Yvonne.

Adam Nordwall was not among this landing party. He was out of town, attending the first National Conference on Indian Education in

Native Americans inspect the prison galleries in the main cell block on Alcatraz Island on November 20, 1969. That day began the long-term occupation of Alcatraz.

A woman paints on a wall at Alcatraz after the November 20, 1969, landing.

Minneapolis, Minnesota. His wife called him there with news of the successful November 20 invasion. "They made it?!" he exclaimed. "Everybody?" Nordwall couldn't wait to inform the educators in Minneapolis. "I have just learned that as many as a hundred Indians landed on Alcatraz this morning," he told the conference attendees. "And this time, they're really there to stay." With that, a thunderous applause echoed through the auditorium.

CHAPTER 6

WE HOLD THE ROCK

"Indians only. If you aren't Indians, please keep going and don't try to land. If you are Indian, welcome to Indian land! Come ashore and join your brothers and sisters."

—Alcatraz Island occupier, announcement
through a loudspeaker, November 1969

After the federal penitentiary closed in 1963, a government agency called the General Services Administration (GSA) had taken charge of Alcatraz. Therefore, it was up to the GSA to deal with the Alcatraz occupation. GSA head Robert Kunzig quickly made plans to remove the trespassers. He would send federal marshals to the island to evict the Indians, by force if necessary. Kunzig's plan never made it off the drawing board, however.

In 1969 Richard Nixon was president of the United States. He had inherited the unpopular war in Vietnam from his predecessor, Lyndon Johnson, and was pursuing that war aggressively. At home in the United States, college campuses simmered with unrest, as student protesters agitated against the war. The protests had turned violent on several occasions, with clashes between police and demonstrators.

Oakland police use mace and batons on anti–Vietnam War protesters during "Stop the Draft Week" in October 1967. Violent protests were common at this time.

At the same time, big U.S. cities also roiled with violence. In one city after another—Los Angeles, Detroit, Baltimore, and many more—African Americans rioted in the streets, demonstrating their anger and frustration with poverty, police brutality, and racial discrimination. They too clashed with police, with bloody and sometimes fatal results.

Nixon knew that sending federal marshals onto Alcatraz could easily result in more violence. And the image of well-armed marshals roughing up idealistic American Indian college students would make for bad public relations. What's more, Alcatraz was only a short distance from UC–Berkeley, one of the most activist campuses in the nation, and even closer to downtown San Francisco, a hippie hotbed. Both Berkeley and San Francisco had witnessed dramatic student unrest with the Third World strikes of 1968–1969. And in November 1969, more than a quarter million young people had gathered at San Francisco's Golden Gate Park for an antiwar rally. The whole region was a countercultural tinderbox. Nixon didn't want to see it ignite.

Assistants to President Nixon told Kunzig to call off his raid. Angered at having his authority yanked, Kunzig turned over all dealings with the occupiers to Tom Hannon, GSA administrator for the San Francisco region. Hannon had already interacted with the occupiers during the first two attempts to take Alcatraz. The White House directed him to negotiate with the Indians.

Hannon arrived on Alcatraz at about four in the afternoon on November 20. He found the island in a frenzy of activity. Reporters had

> "We came to Alcatraz because we were sick and tired of being pushed around, exploited, and degraded everywhere we turned in our country."
>
> —Indians of All Tribes, *statement to the federal government, November 1969*

Coast Guard boats like this one struggled to intercept Indians and their supporters *(background)* in the waters around Alcatraz.

invaded along with the Native Americans. News helicopters swooped overhead. Pleasure boaters cruised near the shore. They cheered on the invaders and tossed them gifts of food and blankets. Curious about the old penitentiary and its infamous former occupants, many non-Indians wanted to come ashore to explore the prison for themselves. But the occupiers wouldn't let them land. Meanwhile, the Coast Guard tried to establish a blockade around the island. But curiosity seekers dodged right past them in their boats.

Hannon met with Richard Oakes, who by then had become the unofficial spokesperson for the invaders. Hannon told Oakes that with its crumbling walkways, barbed wire, and rusty machinery, the island was unsafe—especially for the children who made up part of the occupying force.

Oakes waved off Hannon's concerns. He said the occupiers were prepared to care for themselves. They had food, sleeping bags, and other provisions and had arranged for supply boats to arrive from mainland. They had no intention of leaving Alcatraz. Hannon then told Oakes that everyone needed to leave by noon the following day, but the deadline came and went and the government took no action. It didn't want to force the occupiers to leave the island. It planned to continue to negotiate.

THANKSGIVING

The public response to the Alcatraz invasion—especially from the Bay Area activist community—was overwhelmingly positive. Immediately, donations of food, clothing, blankets, and money began pouring into the San Francisco Indian Center, which had set up temporary headquarters on Sixteenth Street after the fire. Mainland organizers set up a staging area at Pier 40, where they loaded donations onto Alcatraz-bound boats.

Meanwhile, more Indians—young and old, whole families, people from every tribal background—caught boats to the Rock. By the end of

The San Francisco Indian Center operated this receiving facility on Pier 40 to store donations and load them into boats going to Alcatraz.

People cook eggs on the plaza in front of the Alcatraz cell house on the second morning of occupation in November 1969. Supporters immediately began to donate food to help protesters on the island.

the second day of occupation, the population stood at more than 150.

The Coast Guard blockade continued but remained ineffective. As Coast Guard vessels scurried to intercept one boat, other boats would slip past them to the island. Some supporters simply tossed donations onto the Alcatraz dock and sped away. Others delivered supplies beneath the rocky cliffs on the north side of the island. Occupiers then hauled up the supplies via rickety ladders and a human chain. When the Coast Guard did manage to intercept an Alcatraz-bound boat, the punishment was a minor citation, sort of like a traffic ticket. This was not much of a deterrent to those intent on reaching the island. In a few days, the Coast Guard gave up and called off the blockade.

The occupation was less than a week old when Thanksgiving rolled around. At the first New England Thanksgiving, in 1621, about ninety American Indians had joined English colonists for a feast and celebration. The struggling colonists had prepared a fairly meager dinner of game birds, fish, and bread, but the Indians fortified the meal with a gift of five deer. Almost 350 years later on Alcatraz, it was the

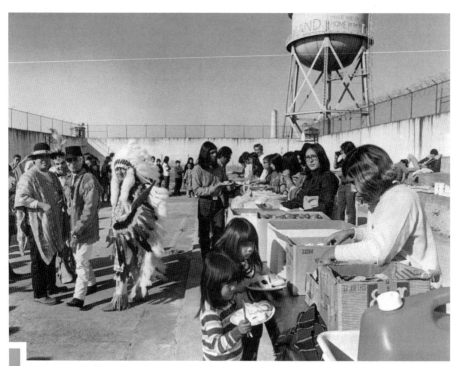

Thanksgiving dinner is served on Alcatraz Island in 1969. Supporters on the mainland supplied the food.

non-Indians who fleshed out the celebration with food. The Bratskeller Restaurant in San Francisco announced that it would cook and deliver a Thanksgiving meal for everyone on the island. Additional mainland contributors sent frozen turkeys ahead of time.

By the time the holiday arrived, the island population had swelled even more. Indian chefs augmented the Bratskeller turkeys and trimmings with platters of fry bread, mutton, venison (deer meat), and corn. Hundreds of Indians, many of them outfitted in traditional dance regalia, enjoyed the feast. Afterward, the occupiers drummed, danced, and sang late into the night.

■ ■ ■ SETTLING IN

The old prison buildings on Alcatraz were run-down but not completely uninhabitable. The island held several single-family homes, apartment houses, and a barracks, which had once housed prison staff. Most occupiers chose to live in these quarters, although some adventurers set up camp in the old cell house. The island had a small supply of cold running water, which came from a water barge tied up along the dock. The Island also had telephone service. Some prison buildings had electric power, but there was no gas for cooking or heating and no refrigerators. A few buildings had fireplaces.

The government had done little building maintenance in the six years the prison had sat empty. Some of the toilets and other plumbing didn't work, so occupiers set about repairing them. They also rewired electrical circuits and patched up a few old prison trucks and got them running.

Quickly, the occupiers realized they'd need some sort of governing body to guide decision making and to deal with the press and federal government.

Occupiers clean up and repair facilities on Alcatraz Island in December 1969. Over time, the occupiers created an organization to run the island smoothly.

John Trudell *(right)* interviews Grace Thorpe (daughter of Olympic athlete Jim Thorpe) on his *Radio Free Alcatraz* broadcast on December 26, 1969. Occupiers set up their own radio station and broadcast for fifteen minutes each evening.

MORE **THORPES**

Jim Thorpe is remembered as one of the greatest athletes of the twentieth century. A member of the Sac and Fox tribe, he won two gold medals in track and field at the 1912 Olympic Games. He later played professional baseball and professional football. Thorpe's daughter Grace is less well known. But she was an Indian activist and a leader in the early months of the Alcatraz occupation. She handled much of the media relations. Grace's daughter and Jim's granddaughter, twenty-two-year-old Dagmar Thorpe, lived on Alcatraz as well. She took care of very young children in the island nursery.

That body was the elected, seven-person All Tribes Council. The first council was made up of six college students, Richard Oakes, Al Miller, Ross Harden, Bob Nelford, Dennis Turner, and James Vaughn, plus UCLA instructor Ed Castillo.

Everyone on the island was welcome at council meetings. Many non-council members participated just as much as the elected representatives. The occupiers strove to make decisions by consensus— that is, by gathering general agreement from everyone at a meeting rather than with a majority-rules voting system. The council had scheduled meetings each Friday, but it actually met much more often to deal with issues as they arose. Sometimes the council met several times a day. The occupiers also established an election system: every ninety days, all the adult occupiers on the island would vote on new council members.

Soon Alcatraz was running smoothly. Everyone performed a job: kitchen work, garbage cleanup, or public relations. Women did most of the cooking, sometimes over big campfires on the dock, sometimes indoors. Men handled island security. They stationed lookouts on top of

"We did a lot of singing in those days. I remember the fires at night-time, the cold of the night, the singing around the campfire . . . the songs of friendship, the songs of understanding. We did a lot of singing. We sang into the early hours of the morning. It was beautiful to behold and beautiful to listen to."

—*Richard Oakes, Alcatraz leader, 1972*

the cell house and other buildings and watched for government boats through binoculars.

Grace Thorpe, daughter of Sac and Fox superathlete Jim Thorpe, handled most of the outreach to the media. Dorothy Lonewolf Miller,

Children play below the lighthouse on Alcatraz. Occupation leaders set up the Big Rock School for them in the main cell house.

a Blackfoot, managed a lot of necessary business from her offices on the mainland. She opened a bank account for the Indians of All Tribes and established a two-way radio link between her office and the island. Sioux nurse Stella Leach set up a health clinic on Alcatraz. She and other Native American nurses staffed the clinic, while several volunteer non-Indian doctors visited regularly from the mainland. Mainland supporters also donated medical supplies.

Increasingly, children were coming to live on Alcatraz. They needed to attend school, so several teachers among the occupying force organized a classroom. Called the Big Rock School, the class met in an assembly hall in the main cell house. The student body consisted of about twelve children, mostly in grades one through six. Although the school was not accredited (approved by the government), San Francisco officials allowed it to remain open and didn't punish any parents for having their children miss school on the mainland. In addition to standard lessons in reading, writing, and math, students at the Big Rock School also learned about Indian culture and history.

Blackfoot artist Earl Livermore, director of the San Francisco Indian Center, also ran a school on Alcatraz. There, he and other artists taught both children and adults traditional Indian crafts such as beadwork, leatherwork, and wood carving. Other occupiers ran a nursery for very young children.

To publicize the occupation, Peter Blue Cloud created the *Indians of All Tribes Newsletter*. The publication featured island news, as well as other items of interest to both Indian and non-Indian readers. Meanwhile, the local newspapers couldn't get enough of the Alcatraz story. Between November 20, 1969, and January 10, 1970, the *San Francisco Chronicle* and the *San Francisco Examiner* published more than 125 articles about Alcatraz. Tim Findley of the *San Francisco Chronicle* filed many of these stories. A non-Indian, Findley was nevertheless a big supporter of the San Francisco Indian community. He had been in on the invasion planning from the start and even helped arrange for the three boats from Sausalito.

As word of the occupation spread, more and more non-Indians offered their support. By then the nation had undergone a social transformation. The media was full of antiwar rhetoric (persuasive language), talk of women's liberation, and discussions about social justice and injustice. Americans were at last awakening to the truth about Native Americans in U.S. history. One man wrote to President Nixon:

I think the Indians taking over Alcatraz is the most refreshing thing that has happened to this country in years, and certainly hope you will find a way to let them have it.

Our treatment of the Indians has been one of the most shameful things in our history, and this is a glorious beginning to what could become something we could be proud of.

Cash donations from non-Indian supporters piled up in the Indians of All Tribes bank account. Comedian Dick Gregory made a large donation. Songwriter Malvina Reynolds penned a tune called "Alcatraz"

Actress Jane Fonda *(seated, second from left)* **and occupier Stella Leach**
(seated, right) **speak to reporters about transferring Alcatraz Island to
Indian control. Many celebrities supported the occupation.**

and also donated money. Native American folksinger Buffy Sainte-
Marie donated fresh water and gave benefit concerts for the occupation.

Creedence Clearwater Revival, a rock band, donated fifteen thousand
dollars toward the purchase of a boat, which the occupiers renamed the
Clearwater. It made regular trips between the island and the mainland.
Volunteer boaters, including the three skippers from Sausalito who had
ferried the November 20 landing force, continued delivering Indians
to the island. In addition to passengers, boats brought donated food,
cooking fuel, and other necessities.

And more Indians kept arriving—some from as far off as Canada and
South America. Many of the urban-based occupiers were accustomed
to socializing and organizing with members of different tribes. Many
rural occupiers, however, met people of different tribes for the first
time when they came to Alcatraz.

Those already established on the island welcomed the newcomers
heartily. A spirit of fellowship filled the air.

The occupation of Alcatraz was seen as daring, noble, and even a little glamorous. Student activists loved the occupiers for their defiance of authority. Many hippies admired the Indians for their ancient religions and traditional lifeways. Previously ignored or ridiculed, all at once American Indians were cool.

Celebrities wanted to visit Alcatraz. Actors Anthony Quinn, Candice Bergen, and Jonathan Winters all arrived in the early weeks of the occupation. Talk show host Merv Griffin came to Alcatraz and broadcast a program about the occupation direct from the island. Actress and antiwar activist Jane Fonda visited the island and made friends with occupier LaNada Boyer. Fonda arranged for Boyer to talk about the occupation on several Los Angeles television shows. Boyer also flew to New York to appear on the popular nationally broadcast Dick Cavett Show.

Some non-Indian supporters wanted to move to Alcatraz and join the occupation. But the occupiers insisted that only Indians be allowed as permanent residents. Grace Thorpe wrote many letters explaining this policy to non-Indians who asked to join the occupation. She thanked them for their support but explained, "I am certain that you understand; this is our first 'free' land since the white man came."

"It was like a home," remembered occupier Denise Quitiquit. "It was like a community. It was like finding yourself again." George Horse Capture concurred: "Riding to the island, the refreshing spray of the bay splashing in my face, I felt, for the first time in decades, as if I belonged, as if I were home."

One teenager from Texas arrived wearing beads and proclaiming that he was a Comanche. Other Comanches were happy to meet a fellow tribe member. But when they quizzed him more about his roots, the young man drew a blank. As it turned out, his Comanche identity was just a few days old. He had been watching news of the occupation on TV with his family and declared: "Gee, I wish I was an Indian. I'd go to Alcatraz." At that point, his mother turned to him and said, "Son, you are an Indian. You're half Comanche." As soon as he heard that, he caught a ride to the island.

Some American Indians joined the occupation for just a weekend or so and then returned home to their jobs and families. Adam Nordwall had to run his business in San Leandro. He visited the island on occasion, including Thanksgiving, but never stayed long. Other Indians settled in to stay. Stella Leach took a three-month leave of absence from her job at the All Indian Well Baby Clinic in Berkeley to join the occupation. John Trudell arrived at Thanksgiving and was so inspired that he packed up his whole family in Los Angeles and moved them to Alcatraz. Some college student occupiers caught the first boat out in the morning, attended classes on the mainland, and returned to Alcatraz at night. The island's total population fluctuated. It swelled to many hundreds on weekends and numbered between fifty and one hundred during the week.

■ ■ ■ BOTTOM LINE

The original goal of the occupiers had been to relocate the San Francisco Indian Center to Alcatraz. But as they planned for it, a more detailed scheme emerged. The occupiers envisioned a large Indian complex on Alcatraz. The complex would include a Native American university, a spiritual center, an ecology center, a vocational (job training) school, an arts and crafts center, and a museum. The specifics were outlined in the Indians of All Tribes proclamation of November 9, 1969.

After initially thinking they would be evicted from (forced off) the island, the occupiers realized that the government instead intended to negotiate with them. So LaNada Boyer and the first All Tribes Council drafted a document outlining the occupiers' main demands. First, they wanted Walter Hickel, U.S. interior secretary, to come to Alcatraz and surrender the island to them personally. The Indians named Hickel because he headed the Department of the Interior, the federal department that runs the BIA. Second, the occupiers wanted the federal government to provide enough money to build the American Indian cultural complex and keep it running. The document also stated that the cultural complex would be staffed and governed solely by Indians—with no interference from any U.S. government agency.

For its part, the federal government still wasn't sure how to handle the Alcatraz occupation. For the first month or so, sitting and waiting seemed like the best plan.

RED
FLAGS

"We'd done enough killing of Indians in the last two hundred years and we weren't about to do any more. Our policy was restraint and negotiation and talk and [to] try to work out some alternatives.[50]"

—Bradley Patterson, White House official, 1970

Along with six others, Richard Oakes sat on the first All Tribes Council. The council was the only official leadership on Alcatraz. There was no hierarchy among council members—no president, vice president, or other officers. But since even before the occupation, Oakes had emerged as the unofficial leader of Alcatraz. He had read the stirring Indians of All Tribes proclamation on November 9, 1969—and had captured the nation's attention in doing so. It was hard not to notice Richard Oakes. He was handsome, strong, confident, and well spoken. Photographers snapped his picture happily. When reporters or government officials came to Alcatraz, they usually sought out Oakes. The press called him the president, mayor, or chief of Alcatraz. They said he looked like the 1940s–1950s movie star Victor Mature.

Richard Oakes *(left)*, Earl Livermore *(center)*, and Al Miller *(right)* talk to the press on December 24, 1969. Early on, the press identified Oakes as the leader of the occupation

But many other occupiers didn't appreciate having Oakes elevated above everyone else. Many didn't know him well and weren't sure they wanted to follow him. And as his face appeared on more and more news broadcasts, some resented his growing celebrity. In addition, some Indians were uncomfortable with the concept of a single leader in general. They preferred a consensus-based style of government—the kind used historically by many American Indian tribes.

Other Indians did not like the All Tribes Council as a whole. They felt loyalty to their own tribes and rejected the idea of a pantribal government on Alcatraz. In fact, early on in the occupation, signs began to appear on various doorways: "Pomo Room! Do Not Disturb," "Sioux Room," or "Lodge of the Cheyenne." Different tribes staked out different territories around the old prison. They allied themselves behind leaders of their own choosing.

RADIO FREE **ALCATRAZ**

The Alcatraz occupation even had its own radio show—*Radio Free Alcatraz*. The show aired for fifteen minutes at seven fifteen every evening from station KPFA in Berkeley. Affiliated stations in Los Angeles and New York also carried the broadcast. Occupier John Trudell hosted the show. He reported on events at Alcatraz, as well as issues facing Indians nationwide. He sometimes broadcast Indian elders telling ancient stories. Other topics included discussions of treaty disputes and other ongoing problems in Indian Country.

After Thanksgiving, many of the college students who had launched the occupation had to leave Alcatraz. They needed to attend classes, write papers, and take exams. Although some commuted back and forth to school by boat, others simply left for good. Meanwhile, the new people who arrived on Alcatraz had fewer commitments on the mainland. Some were unemployed or homeless—they had no reason to leave the island. The newcomers were devoted to the occupation. But they didn't all share the idealism and historic insight of the original student occupiers.

After the majority of students left, the divisions on Alcatraz grew stronger. Different groups had different ideas about how the occupation should be run and who should lead it. Hostility toward Richard Oakes grew stronger as well. Some people even threatened his wife and children. Some occupiers also lashed out at non-Indian visitors to the island. Originally, the student leaders had instituted a "no-drugs, no-alcohol" policy for Alcatraz. But occupiers increasingly ignored the rule.

Reporter Tim Findley had helped plan the occupation. He wanted it to succeed, but he saw it was falling apart. In late December, he wrote a three-part article in the *San Francisco Chronicle* on how the occupation had fallen apart in just one month. He said that the Indian occupiers had given in to "booze, bickering, and boredom." After that, press coverage of Alcatraz fell off. Many non-Indians still supported the occupation, but overall public enthusiasm decreased. Meanwhile, occupiers felt that Findley had betrayed them with negative press.

■ TRAGEDY

A number of families lived on Alcatraz. These included the Oakes family, consisting of Richard, Anne, and their five children. The youngest Oakes child was two. The oldest was twelve-year-old Yvonne. Like most of the families on Alcatraz, the Oakeses lived in an apartment building that had once housed prison staff. The building was several stories tall, with a concrete courtyard at the center.

On January 3, 1970, Yvonne Oakes was playing with other children on the building's third-floor landing. Accounts of the event differ, but somehow Yvonne slipped through a railing and fell three stories, landing on her head on the concrete. She was unconscious but still alive. The panicked occupiers notified authorities on the mainland, who sent in a rescue helicopter. Yvonne spent four days in a San Francisco hospital but died without regaining consciousness.

Yvonne's death left her parents heartbroken. They both also suspected that Richard Oakes's enemies on Alcatraz had had Yvonne pushed off the landing. Later, federal investigators interviewed the

Alcatraz leader Richard Oakes *(left)* unloads food, while his daughter Yvonne flashes a victory sign. Yvonne died as a result of a tragic fall on the island.

children who had seen Yvonne fall. The investigation determined that her death had been an accident, but her parents remained unconvinced. The Oakes family left Alcatraz after the death, and Richard cut his ties with the occupation. He told fellow occupier Al Miller, "You guys, do what you can with it [Alcatraz]. I don't have the heart for it anymore."

PLAN B

With Oakes gone, leadership on the island shifted partly to fifty-year-old Stella Leach. She had earned much respect for running the island health clinic. The other occupiers elected her to the All Tribes Council. Most important, Leach had a strong group of backers—an Indian street gang

Stella Leach, who ran the island health clinic, stepped into the leadership vacuum after Richard Oakes left Alcatraz.

called the Thunderbirds. Made up of bikers, Vietnam vets, and street toughs, the gang was based on the mainland, in Oakland. But a number of its members had moved to Alcatraz, where they took over island security. Wearing army fatigues and red headbands and armbands, they pushed around not only white reporters and other visitors to the island but also any occupiers who disagreed with Leach.

Like Richard Oakes before them, Leach and her faction were determined not to budge from Alcatraz. They declared that they would settle for nothing less than full Indian control of the island, the creation of an Indian cultural center there, and the money to keep it running.

The government was still willing to negotiate—as long as the occupation remained peaceful. But it was increasingly wary of the new, more aggressive leadership on Alcatraz. Officials watched the island situation very closely. The Federal Bureau of Investigation (FBI) sent in pilots to take photographs of the occupiers from low-flying planes. Many Indians suspected that some of their fellow occupiers were government agents.

Some government officials still wanted to forcibly remove the occupiers. The government drew up a secret removal plan, code-named Operation Parks. But it was a backup plan, to be used only if negotiations with the occupiers failed.

■ BACK AND FORTH

The federal government had no intention of turning over the deed (document of ownership) to Alcatraz to the Indian occupiers. The government was not against helping Indians. Many government officials wanted to. In part because of the occupation, top U.S. officials were keenly aware of Native American grievances and wanted to address them somehow.

But officials said that an Indian cultural complex on Alcatraz was the wrong approach. It would take millions of dollars to build new facilities and to restore island infrastructure (basic foundation and utilities). It would take millions more to keep a cultural complex running. Creating an Indian university on the island posed even more obstacles. The government already knew how expensive it was to house people permanently on Alcatraz—that's why it had shut down the prison in 1963. The Nixon administration argued that the large dollar amounts in question "could be much better devoted to meeting the problems of housing, education, health and employment involving large numbers of American Indians in the Bay Area."

Frustrated with the new leadership on Alcatraz, the government asked mainland Indians to form a new umbrella organization to enter into negotiations. By this time, mainland leaders were also upset about the rumored drug use and other negative trends on Alcatraz. They believed that the occupation had lost its sense of purpose and unity. Hoping to work with the government to find a reasonable solution, Adam Nordwall and others created the Bay Area Native American Council, or BANAC. It represented not only the occupiers on Alcatraz but also more than two dozen Indian groups around the Bay Area.

The government then dangled a carrot. In exchange for ending the occupation, it offered BANAC a fifty-thousand-dollar grant to fight poverty among Bay Area Indians. Some BANAC members welcomed the government's offer. They were willing to compromise to win improvements for urban Indians. But when the occupiers on Alcatraz heard about the offer, they grew angry. BANAC didn't control the occupation, they insisted—they did. They accused BANAC of trying to sell them out—betraying the original goals of the occupation in exchange for cash. The occupiers rejected the government's offer.

The government then made a new offer. Would the occupiers leave Alcatraz in exchange for part of an area of downtown San Francisco called Fort Mason? The occupiers would not even consider it.

Occupation or no, the federal government had finally decided what to do with Alcatraz itself. It took back its offer to let the city of San Francisco make the decision. Instead, the government planned to make the island part of the new Golden Gate National Recreation Area. This vast park in the San Francisco area would stretch along the Pacific coastline for nearly 60 miles (97 km).

In late March 1970, the government again approached the occupiers. What if it established Alcatraz as a special park within the recreation area—a park dedicated to Native American culture and history? The government plan included an Indian museum and cultural center, monuments to famous American Indians, and a mostly Indian staff. The occupiers again said no. They wanted Alcatraz and the Indian cultural complex on their own terms. They did not want to be part of a government-run park.

The rejection of the Golden Gate proposal was rooted in a deep mistrust of the U.S. government. It was based on hundreds of years of broken treaties and broken promises. Sioux John Trudell declared at a press conference:

> The U.S. government speaks and has spoken in the past of having Indian people control their own lives and their own destiny. And yet the proposal that we submitted to the U.S. government concerning Alcatraz was rejected. Not only was it turned down it was never considered. In [government negotiator] Mr. Robertson's statement he said that they considered the proposal and rejected it because it was unfeasible. All that we get out of this meeting with the U.S. government and their representative is that they are going to continue to do as they have done in the past—which is to do our thinking for us and run things their way.

The occupiers said they were willing to negotiate only on "money and the time and the day that they [the government] will turn over the deed to this island. That is all that is negotiable."

■ SHOWDOWN

When the occupiers rejected the Golden Gate park proposal, the government decided to play hardball. The occupiers got running water for cooking, drinking, and washing from the water barge that sat tied up on the Alcatraz dock. At the end of May, the Coast Guard hauled the barge away. The government also cut off the island's phone service and electricity. With that move, the lighthouse on Alcatraz went dark, as did

> "For the first time since the [Battle of the] Little Bighorn [in 1876], the Indian people, instead of passively withdrawing and accepting their fate, had stepped forward in the bright sunshine and let it be known that they were Indian and proud, and their present situation must and would change."
>
> —George Horse Capture, an Alcatraz occupier, Gros Ventre tribe, 1991

the houses and other prison buildings. Two foghorns that warned ships away from the island also stopped working.

But the occupiers were ready to make do. Supporters had donated gasoline-powered generators to run lights and machinery. The occupiers could also use water shipped in from the mainland. They would not be moved.

CHAPTER 8

FIRE
AND
WATER

It is long past time that the Indian policies of the Federal government began to recognize and build upon the capacities and insights of the Indian people. . . . The time has come to break decisively with the past and to create the conditions for a new era in which the Indian future is determined by Indian acts and Indian decisions.

—President Richard Nixon, July 8, 1970

If the government thought the American Indian community was growing weary of the Alcatraz occupation, it was wrong. In the spring of 1970, the occupiers seemed more determined than ever to continue their protest. They looked forward to more new residents that summer. Many college students planned to return to the island when the spring semester ended.

On Memorial Day weekend, hundreds of Indians showed up at Alcatraz for a powwow. They called the event Indian Liberation Day. During the powwow, the occupiers drafted a Declaration of the Return of Indian Land, written on a piece of sheepskin. It stated in part, "We announce on behalf of all Indian people, or tribes that from this day forward we shall exercise dominion [rule over], and all rights of use and possession over Alcatraz Island in San Francisco Bay."

Later that weekend, a series of fires broke out on Alcatraz. No one knows who set them. The government suspected Indians, and the

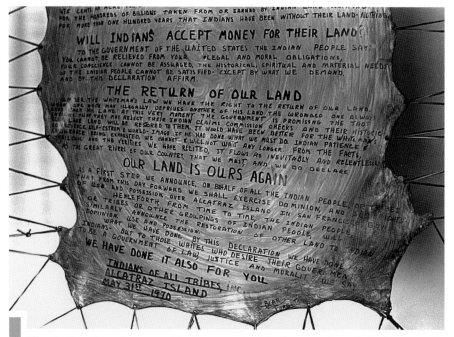

The Native Americans on Alcatraz wrote this Declaration of the Return of Indian Land on May 31, 1970.

A fire that started on Memorial Day weekend 1970 damaged and destroyed a number of island buildings.

Indians suspected government agents. Soon the three-story warden's house and the lighthouse were in flames. With their limited water supplies, the occupiers couldn't do much to fight the fires. The Coast Guard arrived, but the occupiers, wary of a government plot, wouldn't let them on the island. With everyone at a safe distance, the occupiers simply let the buildings burn. When the flames died down, the warden's house and two other structures were gutted. The lighthouse was badly damaged.

Already decrepit when the occupation began, Alcatraz had become even more barren and forbidding. Without running water, the toilets wouldn't flush and sewage backed up. GSA administrator Tom Hannon called Alcatraz "an island ghetto."

SPIN-OFFS

To some it appeared that the occupation was a failure, with nothing positive gained in more than half a year. But in fact, the occupation was sending out ripples across the United States. Inspired by Alcatraz, more and more Indians were staging similar actions.

In mid-June 1970, members of the Pit River Tribe in northern California began an encampment to reclaim 3.5 million acres (1.4 million hectares) of land taken by the federal government in 1853. A number of Alcatraz veterans, including Richard Oakes and Grace Thorpe, traveled north to offer assistance. Wary of another long standoff like that occurring on Alcatraz, the authorities quickly ended the Pit River occupation. They arrested sixty occupiers and took them to jail.

But that protest and others made headlines. Because of Alcatraz, the U.S. public no longer simply ignored American Indian activists or mocked them for "going on the warpath." Reporters started to reveal stories of bleak poverty, high unemployment, and poor public health on Indian reservations—and what might be done to help solve such problems. The public had finally started taking American Indians seriously.

The book *Bury My Heart at Wounded Knee* (1970) is a history of the American West written by Native American historian Dee Brown.

Several books further awakened Americans to the plight and mistreatment of Indians. In *Our Brother's Keeper: The Indian in White America*, legal scholar Edgar S. Cahn exposed the BIA's failure to adequately protect the welfare of Indian people. *Custer Died for Your Sins*, by Indian activist and scholar Vine Deloria Jr., explained how U.S. Indian policy had systematically damaged and demeaned (put down) Native American cultures over hundreds of years. *Bury My Heart at Wounded Knee,* by historian Dee Brown, chronicled the western wars of the 1800s, which marked the final conquest of Indians in North America.

BUFFY SAINTE-MARIE

Singer-songwriter Buffy Sainte-Marie was a major supporter of the Alcatraz occupation. She performed benefit concerts to raise money for the occupiers and also made personal donations. Sainte-Marie was born on a Cree reservation in Saskatchewan, Canada. She was orphaned as a baby and adopted by a Massachusetts family of mixed native and white descent. She graduated from the University of Massachusetts in 1962. Then she found herself at the forefront of both the New York City folk music scene and the peace movement. Her song "Universal Soldier" became an anthem for 1960s antiwar protesters. She also wrote songs about injustices endured by Native American peoples in North America. One such song, "Now That the Buffalo's Gone," talked about broken treaties and the theft of American Indian lands.

Musician Buffy Sainte-Marie performed concerts to raise money for the occupiers of Alcatraz.

A FRIEND IN WASHINGTON

Native Americans found an unlikely ally in the president of the United States. By 1970 the bulk of antiwar protesters, civil rights activists, and other liberal thinkers detested Richard Nixon. He had expanded the unpopular war in Vietnam by illegally bombing Cambodia. He regularly sneered at antiwar activists and hippies, whom he called bums. In the wake of inner city riots and campus protests, he vowed to restore law and order to the United States.

It seemed improbable that Nixon would in any way defend the occupiers on Alcatraz or their supporters. But Nixon had a soft spot for Native Americans. As a student at Whittier College in California, Nixon had become close to his football coach, Wallace Newman. Newman had grown up on the La Jolla Reservation near San Diego, California, and often boasted of his American Indian heritage. Nixon developed a

Richard Nixon *(top center)* is pictured with other members of the Whittier College football team in 1930. Nixon admired and respected the team's Native American coach.

lifelong friendship with Newman. He credited his coach with instilling in him the values of hard work, hard training, and preparation for upcoming challenges. His friendship with Newman made Nixon particularly sympathetic to Indian concerns.

On July 8, 1970, Nixon addressed Congress. His speech signaled a dramatic change in U.S. Indian policy. It began:

> The first Americans—the Indians—are the most deprived and most isolated group in our nation. On virtually every scale of measurement—employment, income, education, health—the condition of the Indian people ranks at the bottom.
>
> This condition is the heritage of centuries of injustice. From the time of the first contact with European settlers, the American Indians have been oppressed and brutalized, deprived of their ancestral lands and denied the opportunity to control their own destiny.

Nixon went on to say that the time had come for change. He announced a multifaceted (many-sided) plan to improve life for Native Americans. The proposal included an end to the termination program, which Nixon denounced fiercely in his speech. He also proposed increased funding for education, economic development, and health care on reservations and increased funding for programs for urban Indians. Nixon further said that American Indian people should have more control within their own communities. Rather than having outside administrators run all BIA programs on reservations, Nixon suggested that tribes should be allowed to run some of these programs if they chose. Such an approach would bring jobs to Indian Country, Nixon explained. He also said that Indian-run programs would likely be more responsive to Indian needs than those run by non-Indians.

Finally, Nixon discussed a ruling by the Indian Claims Commission. The commission had determined that in 1906 the federal government had wrongfully taken 48,000 acres (19,425 hectares) of mountain wilderness in northern New Mexico from the Tiwa Indians. This land included Blue Lake, which is sacred to the Tiwa people. In the past, the

At Taos Pueblo in New Mexico, people gather in the rain to celebrate the return of sacred Blue Lake to the Tiwa people in August 1971.

government would have simply paid off the Indians in cash (in 1906 prices) after the ruling. But Nixon announced that the government would actually return the land to the Tiwa community, Taos Pueblo. This was a first.

Congress supported Nixon's ideas, and many of his proposals became law. The new programs pumped an extra $100 million into American Indian communities. The Blue Lake decision also paved the way for additional lands to be returned to Indian people: 40 million acres (16 million hectares) to the Navajo in the Southwest, 21,000 acres (8,500 hectares) to the Yakima in Washington State, and 60,000 acres (24,282 hectares) to the Warm Springs tribe in Oregon. The relationship between American Indians and the federal government had truly begun to change.

Lou Trudell moved to Alcatraz with her husband, John, and two daughters in late 1969. In July 1970, Lou gave birth to a baby boy on Alcatraz. A doctor and a midwife arrived from the mainland to deliver the baby. The Trudells named him Wovoka, after a Paiute religious leader of the same name. In 1890 Wovoka had founded the Ghost Dance religion in Nevada. He said that by doing the Ghost Dance, followers could bring dead Indians and bison back to life—thus restoring and reviving Indian culture. The religion spread quickly among American Indians living on western reservations. The new religion made U.S. military officials nervous and thousands of solders were sent to the Standing Rock reservation. Sitting Bull, chief of the Sioux, was arrested and accidently killed for failure to control the movement. Soldiers forced Big Foot, another Sioux Leader, and his people to the Pine Ridge Agency to better control them. Then they slaughtered them as they camped at Wound Knee Creek.

STILL WAITING

But on Alcatraz during that summer of 1970 very little had changed. The government and the occupiers remained at a standoff. By then, Stella Leach had returned to her job and home on the mainland. John Trudell and LaNada Boyer emerged as the new leaders of the occupation.

A number of students came and went throughout the summer. American Indian activists from across the country also visited the island. But the more aggressive bikers and street people made up the bulk of island residents. Increasingly, there were signs and stories of violence on Alcatraz. In August an unknown occupier shot an arrow at a passing tour boat. The Coast Guard also reported hostile confrontations with occupiers.

By then public enthusiasm for Alcatraz had cooled greatly. Fewer and fewer donations came in to the San Francisco Indian Center. The government kept up its close surveillance of the island. The FBI continued taking photographs from aircraft. It also hired private citizens living in high-rise apartments on the mainland to watch the island through high-powered telescopes and to report on their observations. The government still had a removal plan—Operation Parks—ready for activation.

The occupiers remained firm in their demands for an American Indian cultural complex, including an Indian university. They named it Thunderbird University—in honor of the Oakland gang members. The occupiers even hired an architectural firm to create preliminary drawings and models of the proposed complex. It included residences based on traditional American Indian homes, such as Iroquois longhouses, Plains Indian tepees, and Navajo hogans.

Meanwhile, outside Alcatraz, Indian activism surged. In early August 1970, Puyallup Indians began a fish-in in Washington State. Later that month, United Native Americans set up an encampment at Mount Rushmore in the Black Hills of the Midwest, demanding the return of more than 100,000 acres (40,500 hectares) to the Sioux. By early September, dozens of other protests were ongoing or in the works.

PLAN C

Also in September, the government was ready to go with Operation Parks. It was a secret mission involving helicopters, boats, and armed U.S. marshals. It was designed to catch the Indian occupiers by surprise. However, *San Francisco Chronicle* columnist Herb Caen got wind of the plan and revealed it to the public in the newspaper. After that, the government denied that it had such a plan.

Tipped off by Caen, the Alcatraz security force scanned the sky and water for a government invasion. They placed metal fuel drums in open spaces on the island to prevent government helicopters from landing there. Operation Parks was no longer viable. It was no longer secret. If enacted, it might create a violent confrontation—with bloody results. It would also be embarrassing to the government to first deny that it had such a plan and then to carry it out. Operation Parks was scrapped.

November 9, 1970, was the one-year anniversary of the first, abbreviated invasion of Alcatraz. This was the day when Richard Oakes and the others had swum to the island from the *Monte Cristo*. Organizers on the mainland held a festive anniversary celebration that more than one thousand attended. On Alcatraz the occupiers held a more serious commemoration later in the month. They called a press conference, restated their plans for an American Indian cultural complex, and presented the architectural drawings. They also restated their determination to remain on the island until their demands were met.

Meanwhile, Indian activism continued to grow. On Thanksgiving Day 1970, activists from the Minneapolis-based American Indian

John Trudell *(center)* speaks with the media about negotiations with the federal government over ownership of Alcatraz Island. The occupation marked its one-year anniversary in November 1970.

On Thanksgiving 1970, AIM activists seized the *Mayflower II*—a replica of the original *Mayflower*—to protest the European colonization of the Americas.

Movement (AIM) went to Plymouth, Massachusetts. This historic town is where the English ship *Mayflower* landed on December 21, 1620. The ship carried the Pilgrims—some of the first European settlers in North America. In 1970 the *Mayflower II*—a replica ship and a tourist attraction—sat at the dock at Plymouth. The AIM activists briefly seized it in a symbolic protest of European colonization of North America. They also proclaimed Thanksgiving to be a national day of mourning for lost American Indian lands.

The lighthouse on Alcatraz, in operation since 1854, was crucial to safe shipping in the Golden Gate area. When the government shut off electricity on Alcatraz, in late May 1970, the lighthouse, as well as its accompanying foghorns, stopped working. The fire a few days later damaged the powerful lightbulb inside the lighthouse but did not destroy the structure.

As a replacement to aid navigation, the Coast Guard installed a string of floating buoys around Alcatraz. Each buoy had its own small beacon—sort of like a mini-lighthouse. The buoys guided boaters around the island. But people in San Francisco missed the steady sweep of the old lighthouse beacon across the horizon at night. The light was part of the cityscape, and many residents were angry when it went dark.

Scott Newhall, editor in chief of the *San Francisco Chronicle*, missed the beacon so much that he arranged to replace the damaged bulb. He sent out a generator to supply the needed electricity. He also sent out an electrician to make the repairs. The lighthouse shone again—but not for long. The occupiers didn't want to divert their much-needed fuel to power Newhall's generator, so they soon let the light go dark again.

Meanwhile, mariners (sailers) began to complain that the floating buoys were not adequate for safe sailing and shipping through the Golden Gate (the sea passage into San Francisco Bay). The Coast Guard desperately wanted the occupation ended or at least for technicians to be sent to Alcatraz to restore power to the lighthouse and foghorns.

In August 1970, John Trudell made the government an offer. The Coast Guard could fix and restore power to the lighthouse and foghorns only if it also returned the water barge and restored electricity to other island buildings as well. If the Coast Guard came to fix only its own equipment, Trudell said, the occupiers would not let their boats land. The government refused to budge on this offer, so the light stayed dark.

Meanwhile, the Coast Guard and boaters continued to complain about safety. In January 1971, two oil tankers collided about a 0.25 mile (0.4 km) outside the Golden Gate, dumping 800,000 gallons (3 million liters) of crude oil into the ocean. The collision had nothing to do with Alcatraz or its navigational buoys. But it reminded the public that a similar accident could happen if the Alcatraz lighthouse stayed dark. The Coast Guard pushed the White House even harder to end the occupation.

Without a working lightbulb inside the Alcatraz lighthouse after May 1970, the lighthouse remained dark. Occupiers and the U.S. government could not agree on a repair plan.

CHAPTER 9

"IF NOT ALCATRAZ, SOMEPLACE ELSE"

Alcatraz is not an island. It's an inspiration. It's the idea that you can recapture your own destiny, and self-determine your own future."

—Richard Oakes, Mohawk and Alcatraz leader, circa 1970

Winter came and went on Alcatraz. The remaining thirty or so islanders scraped by with meager supplies of donated water, fuel, and food. They ate canned beans and hauled heavy water containers up the island's rocky hillsides. They even tore down some prison buildings and burned the boards for firewood.

In April 1971, *Time* magazine printed an article about Alcatraz, which many non-Indian Americans had by then forgotten. "The conditions uncomfortably suggest a typical Indian reservation— isolated, neglected, and barren," the writer said. He continued:

> On cold, windy bay nights the only source of heat is wood planking stripped from the few island structures that have not been destroyed by accidental fires. Most of the toilet plumbing . . . is rusted or jammed and sanitation standards are perilously low. The volunteer nurse has left the island, and the only school has been shut (nearly half of the inhabitants are children under the age of twelve). The island's single truck has broken down.

The writer noted that "the original invasion leaders . . . have been replaced by homeless, apolitical young Indians more concerned with finding a pad [home] where they can 'get their heads together' than in sustaining any kind of significant political statement."

Thomas Scott, a GSA official, offered a similar assessment. He remarked that the original occupiers had been "articulate and very intelligent. . . . At first [the occupiers] were so excited, charged up with a real cause. Later, they didn't seem to know what the cause was or why they were here."

Back on the mainland, most Indian activists thought it was long past time to move on from Alcatraz. Adam Nordwall told the press, "The purpose of occupying Alcatraz was to start an Indian movement and call attention to Indian problems. . . . It has served its purpose." Of the early leadership, only John Trudell and LaNada Boyer were left on the island. They remained defiant. "You can be certain we will not leave Alcatraz," Trudell said that spring. "We have come too far and through too much to start giving back to the white man."

■ ■ ■ REMOVAL

On April 19, 1971, the boat *Clearwater*, purchased the year before with funds from Creedence Clearwater Revival, mysteriously sank at the Alcatraz dock. No one knows what caused the sinking, although some occupiers suspected the U.S. government. By then the occupiers were out of money and could not buy or charter another boat. They had to hitch rides to and from the island on passing boats. The island population continued to dwindle. Based on surveillance data, the government thought that only eleven to fifteen occupiers remained. But it knew that summer could bring a new infusion of college student residents—and possibly renewed public support for the occupation. It was finally time to remove the occupiers.

In early June 1971, the order came from John Ehrlichman, aide to President Nixon. "Go!" With that, heavily armed U.S. marshals

Federal agents arrive on Alcatraz Island to remove the occupiers in June 1971.

When they arrived back in San Francisco, the final fifteen occupiers of Alcatraz remained determined to fight for Indian rights.

from San Francisco, Sacramento, and San Diego descended on Alcatraz in three Coast Guard vessels and one helicopter. On the island, they encountered six men, four women, and five children. The remaining leaders, John Trudell and LaNada Boyer, were not among this group. They were away on the mainland, trying to drum up new support for the occupation.

When the marshals arrived, the fifteen occupiers offered no resistance. They quietly boarded the boats that had come to retrieve them. At a nearby island, officials fed the occupiers lunch and questioned them. Finally, the government put the occupiers up in a San Francisco hotel for one night and then let them go—with no charges filed.

After nineteen months and nine days, the Alcatraz occupation was officially over. But one of the final fifteen, Vicki Lee, told reporters, "We will return to Alcatraz, if not Alcatraz, someplace else."

■ SOMEPLACE ELSE

After the occupation ended, the government sent workers with bulldozers and a wrecking ball to clean up Alcatraz. The workers knocked down some of the least stable structures, including the apartment buildings where most of the occupiers had lived. The operation also wiped out much of the graffiti and other traces of the occupation. The government

Guard John Geagan and his dog Whiskey patrol Alcatraz as a wrecking ball takes down buildings on July 23, 1971.

protected the island from any future invasions with round-the-clock security patrols and guard dogs.

The Alcatraz occupation was no more, but American Indian activism was by then at full strength around the United States. During the course of the nineteen-month Alcatraz occupation, Indian activists had carried out thirty-six other protests across the nation.

After the occupation, the protest movement kept going strong. These are just a few of dozens of examples: In June 1971, an activist group threatened to hold the Statue of Liberty hostage to protest the poor treatment of Native Americans. On July 4, 1971, AIM occupied Mount Rushmore National Monument in South Dakota and declared a Fourth of July countercelebration. In August AIM members seized an abandoned Coast Guard lifeboat station in Milwaukee, Wisconsin— claiming rights to the property under the Sioux Treaty of 1868. In September the Denver chapter of AIM occupied the Anthropology Department at Colorado State University and symbolically arrested a professor and seven students. The protesters objected to a standard practice in anthropology: digging up sacred Native American graves to study the skeletal remains. The activists called the anthropologists grave robbers and declared that dead Indian ancestors should be left in peace.

TURNING UP THE HEAT

By this time, AIM had emerged as the leading Indian activist group in the nation. AIM founders Dennis Banks and Clyde Bellecourt, along with Russell Means (a veteran of the 1964 invasion of Alcatraz), were the group's most prominent members. They became the spokespeople for the new American Indian activism sweeping the United States.

When AIM took action, the press and the government took notice. In October 1972, AIM and the NIYC carried out the most visible protest since Alcatraz. In an action called the Trail of Broken Treaties, more than two thousand protesters drove from across the nation to Washington, D.C. The group had drafted a twenty-point plan that would redefine the relationship between American Indian tribes and the U.S. government. The protesters wanted to present the document to President Nixon.

Dennis Banks *(left)* **protests with preacher Carl McIntire** *(right)* **on November 4, 1972, during the Trail of Broken Treaties demonstration.**

When plans for housing the protesters in Washington, D.C., fell through, the group took over BIA headquarters, evicted the staff, and held the building for more than a week. The occupation quickly turned ugly. Occupiers smashed windows and bathroom fixtures, rifled through BIA documents, and covered walls with graffiti. They also soaked furniture and office equipment with gasoline—preparing to set the whole place aflame if the authorities came in to forcibly remove them. The action ended peacefully, with no arrests, but the occupiers had done more than $2 million in damages to the building. Indian activism was becoming more confrontational.

Then the federal government turned up the heat on AIM. Government officials described AIM leaders as terrorists, revolutionaries, and "mad dogs." The FBI set out to neutralize the group—to see that it carried out no more effective political activities.

The growing hostility between AIM and the U.S. government came to a head on the Pine Ridge Sioux Reservation in South Dakota in 1973.

After leaving Alcatraz following his daughter's death, Richard Oakes returned to school at San Francisco State. He didn't give up his activism. In March 1970, he led a sit-in at a BIA office near Oakland. In early June, he joined the Indian protesters at Pit River in California.

After returning to San Francisco, Oakes's life took another tragic turn. One night he got into a fight at a bar. Someone smacked him in the head with a pool cue, knocking him out. Friends carried him home and told his wife he was drunk, not mentioning the head injury. But in the morning, Anne was unable to wake him. It turned out he had a fractured skull and needed surgery. Afterward, he remained in a coma in the hospital for one month. Three American Indian medicine men visited Oakes in the hospital. They treated him with prayers and herbs. Much to his doctors' surprise, he awakened and recovered much sooner than expected.

That September Oakes embarked on a new journey. He, Anne, and their children set out in an old school bus to tour reservations and other Indian communities. They planned to conduct a "traveling college" on American Indian issues. The bus soon broke down, however, and Oakes turned his attention to other ventures. Over the next few years, he tried various moneymaking activities and activist projects. One idea was for Indians to start deer ranches to produce venison for sale.

In September 1972, Oakes landed in the middle of a dispute between security guards and Indian youths at a YMCA camp north of San Francisco. One guard thought Oakes was about to draw a weapon. The guard shot Oakes in the chest, killing him. Oakes had been unarmed, but a court later ruled that the guard had fired in self-defense. The killing enraged the American Indian activist community and partly inspired the 1972 Trail of Broken Treaties occupation of BIA headquarters in Washington, D.C.

As at other reservations, Pine Ridge had a tribal government that worked closely with the BIA. The tribal president was a man named Richard Wilson. Many tribal members disliked Wilson. They said he was corrupt, made dishonest land deals with the federal government, handed out reservation jobs to his relatives, and was more indebted to the BIA than to his own Sioux people. Wilson even ran a military-style police force, Guardians of the Oglala Nation (known as GOON), to intimidate his political enemies. Tribal members filed formal complaints against Wilson with the BIA. But the agency ignored their concerns. They complained to the Justice Department and the FBI—also with no results. Finally, the tribal members turned to AIM for help.

Russell Means, Dennis Banks, and two hundred other AIM members arrived at the reservation to assess the situation. They found not only GOON but also armed U.S. marshals and BIA police waiting to confront them. The government intended to use the showdown at Pine Ridge to destroy AIM. It even had army troops ready to move in from Fort Carson, Colorado, if necessary.

Equally determined to fight federal authorities, AIM members were equipped with weapons of their own. They dug in at the reservation village of Wounded Knee, near the sight of the 1890 massacre. Federal forces surrounded the AIM position and waited, trying to starve out the defenders by cutting off their food supply. But despite the blockade, supporters from the reservation sneaked into the AIM camp at night with food and ammunition.

AIM held its position for seventy-one days, occasionally taking gunfire from federal forces—and occasionally returning fire. The shooting resulted in two Indian deaths and several injuries, as well as injuries to two federal troops. Finally, on May 7, 1973, negotiators for the two sides reached an agreement, ending the standoff. The FBI then arrested more than five hundred AIM members on charges related to Wounded Knee. The arrests sent AIM into disarray. Members spent so much time defending themselves in court that they were unable to carry out the other work of the organization. Only fifteen AIM members ended up with convictions after the standoff. It appeared, however, as though the FBI had effectively neutralized AIM as planned.

American Indian Movement (AIM) members guard a roadblock outside Wounded Knee on the Pine Ridge Reservation in South Dakota on March 3, 1973.

But AIM eventually regrouped. In 1975 it returned to Pine Ridge to continue the fight against GOON, as well as against their FBI and BIA police backers. This time, the group set up defensive encampments at key spots around the reservation. On June 26, 1975, two federal agents fired on an AIM camp near the village of Oglala. AIM fighters returned fire, killing the two agents. That night the government swept in with helicopters and heavy artillery. The AIM combatants had fled by then.

With the killings of the two agents, the FBI increased its anti-AIM campaign. Although about thirty AIM members had fired on the agents, the FBI picked out four leaders as the likely killers. One of them, Leonard Peltier, fled to northern Alberta, Canada, where he took refuge with a group of Cree Indians. The government proceeded with charges against two of the others but dropped charges against the fourth. Meanwhile,

Guards escort AIM member Leonard Peltier from a Canadian prison in December 1976. He returned to the United States to face charges of murdering FBI agents at Wounded Knee.

federal agents found Peltier and brought him back to the United States.

At trial in 1976, a jury returned a not guilty verdict for Peltier's two codefendants. The jury concluded that the men had acted in self-defense. But at a separate trial eight months later (which many say was rigged), another jury found Peltier guilty of the two killings. The judge sentenced him to serve two life terms in prison.

The FBI had finally achieved its goals. After Leonard Peltier's conviction, AIM was pretty much crippled. Many of its leaders were dead or in prison. The organization faded from the national scene. Eight years after the Alcatraz takeover, American Indian activism seemed to have sputtered out.

THE LONGEST WALK

But it was not over. American Indians still held valuable land—rich in minerals and timber—that many powerful U.S. business interests wanted. The way to get this land, some reasoned, was to weaken existing laws that protected American Indian treaty rights and Indian self-governance. In 1978 business lobbyists (people who work to convince government officials of their clients, point of view) persuaded legislators to introduce eleven bills into Congress. The eleven pieces of legislation would have cancelled treaties, taken back Indian fishing and water rights, shut down Indian schools and hospitals, and weakened tribal self-government.

Once again, it was time for action. American Indian leaders organized an event called the Longest Walk—a 3,600-mile (5,792 km) trek across the United States from California to Washington, D.C. The marchers intended to protest the proposed legislation. But their walk also symbolized numerous forced marches of American Indian peoples to Indian Territory and to reservations, such as the Trail of Tears in 1838–1839 and the Long Walk of the Navajos in 1864.

On February 11, 1978, a handful of walkers set out from Sacramento, California. The marchers covered more than 20 miles (32 km) a day, sometimes enduring storms and bitter cold. They camped along the road at night. As they moved from town to town, both Indians and non-Indians joined the march. Supporters offered donations of food, camping gear, medical supplies, and clothing. Most marchers traveled with the group for only a few days or a week, but some logged thousands of miles cross-country. By the time they reached Washington, D.C., on July 15, the group was several thousand strong. The march had generated tremendous public support. March

On February 11, 1978, more than three hundred marchers, including Indian leaders Dennis Banks *(left)* and Max Bear *(center)*, leave Sacramento, California, to kick off the Longest Walk. The cross-country trek protested laws that would have weakened Native American rights.

leader Lehman Brightman, a founder of United Native Americans and by then a college professor, described the arrival in Washington, D.C.:

> This walk was one of the proudest activities that I have ever taken part in. When we came into Washington, D.C., I felt twenty feet [6 meters] high. As we walked into the suburbs, there were thousands of people along the way cheering us on. They offered juice and water and they had signs out that said, "We love Indians!"
>
> You can't imagine the lump in your throat that comes with people cheering you on like that—particularly when you know you have just completed an impossible task.
>
> What a sight—to see those old people and young people all walking so proud, marching four abreast, singing their hearts out, and all the banners flying.

The Longest Walk was a success on many levels. For one thing, the eleven bills in question never got serious consideration in Congress. At the same time, the march reenergized the Native American community and refocused the nation's attention on the needs and concerns of Indian people. It was the biggest Native American action since Alcatraz.

CHAPTER 10

AMERICAN INDIAN
RENAISSANCE

"Our people sacrificed a lot to come here, to give a message to the U.S. government that the Indian people have a right to be . . . who they are."

—William Means, Sioux leader, 2009

In 1972 the National Park Service (NPS) officially took over Alcatraz. The island became part of the Golden Gate National Recreation Area. Construction workers arrived to repair and renovate the dilapidated prison buildings. In 1973 the island officially opened to tourists.

The island didn't become a special park to honor Native Americans, as the government had proposed during the long-drawn-out negotiations with occupiers. Instead, Alcatraz became a prison museum. Tour guides took visitors through the solitary confinement cells, death row, and other spooky prison areas. The tourists learned about Robert Stroud—the famous Birdman of Alcatraz—and other prisoners who had once been locked up there. Visitors even learned a little about the American Indian occupation. The NPS had left some of the occupiers' red power graffiti in place, and guides mentioned the occupation in their tours. Alcatraz soon became one of the most popular tourist spots in California.

Some of the graffiti from the days of the Alcatraz occupation can still be seen on Alcatraz Island.

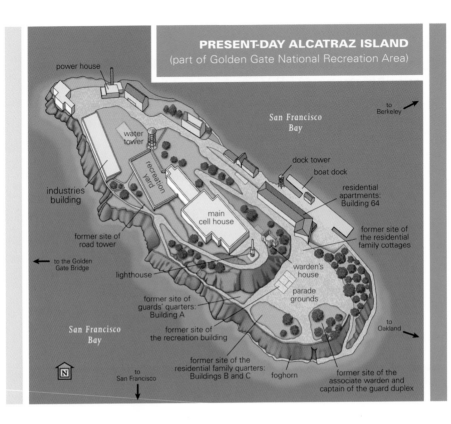

PRESENT-DAY ALCATRAZ ISLAND
(part of Golden Gate National Recreation Area)

power house

San Francisco Bay

to Berkeley

water tower

dock tower

boat dock

recreation yard

residential apartments: Building 64

industries building

main cell house

former site of road tower

former site of the residential family cottages

to the Golden Gate Bridge

lighthouse

warden's house

former site of guards' quarters: Building A

parade grounds

San Francisco Bay

former site of the recreation building

to Oakland

N

to San Francisco

former site of the residential family quarters: Buildings B and C

foghorn

former site of the associate warden and captain of the guard duplex

THE FIGHT GOES ON

As the years went by, many non-Indians forgot about the Alcatraz occupation. But Native Americans did not forget. They carried the spirit of the occupation with them into the political activism of the following years and decades.

The late twentieth century saw many important legal victories for Native Americans. In 1978 Congress passed the American Indian Religious Freedom Act. This law states that American Indian religions and religious ceremonies are protected by the First Amendment to the U.S. Constitution. The Native American Language Act of 1990 provides for funds and programs to help preserve Indian languages in the United States. The Native American Graves Protection and Repatriation Act, also of 1990, requires that federally funded agencies and museums return human Indian remains and sacred objects to tribes.

Native Americans continued protests and kept up the pressure to have their history and heritage respected. In the early 1990s, they protested against sports teams with demeaning Indian names, such as the Washington Redskins. They challenged demeaning Indian mascots, such as the grinning, red-faced mascot of the Cleveland Indians. The protests pressured some but not all teams to make changes.

Since the mid-twentieth century, many American Indians had protested the celebration of Columbus Day. This national holiday honors the man whose landing in the Americas ultimately led to the death of millions of American Indian peoples. The year 1992 marked the quincentenary (five-hundredth anniversary) of Columbus's voyage. Much of the United States held a big celebration, complete with parades, speeches, and reenactments. But across the nation, Native Americans marked the anniversary with protests and countercelebrations. Many called the quincentenary a day of mourning for all the American

On Columbus Day in 1992, many Americans celebrated the five-hundredth anniversary of Columbus's first voyage to the Americas. At the same time, many Native Americans held countercelebrations.

Indians victimized since the first European landing in the Americas.

Modern Indians still have much work to do. In the twenty-first century, Indian people still suffer from high rates of poverty, unemployment, and health problems. But thanks to the work of the Alcatraz occupiers and others, U.S. society finally understands the reality of Indian history and tries to honor Native Americans. Modern school textbooks present a more accurate view of the history of white–Indian relations. "Cowboy and Indian" movies have given way to more accurate screen depictions of Native American history and culture.

Perhaps the most visible tribute to Native Americans in modern times is the National Museum of the American Indian (NMAI). Congress created the NMAI in 1989. In 2004 the museum moved into

UN-THANKSGIVING

Every year in November, American Indians return to Alcatraz to celebrate an "Un-Thanksgiving" and to commemorate the 1969 occupation. The event always features traditional costumes, singing, drumming, and dancing. The 2009 Un-Thanksgiving marked the fortieth anniversary of the occupation. At a sunrise ceremony on the island that year, AIM leader William Means, whose brother Russell and father, Walter, had laid claim to Alcatraz in 1964, addressed the crowd:

We want this place [Alcatraz] listed on the sacred sites of North America. Our people sacrificed a lot to come here, to give a message to the U.S. government that the Indian people have a right to be . . . who they are, that John Wayne didn't kill us all.

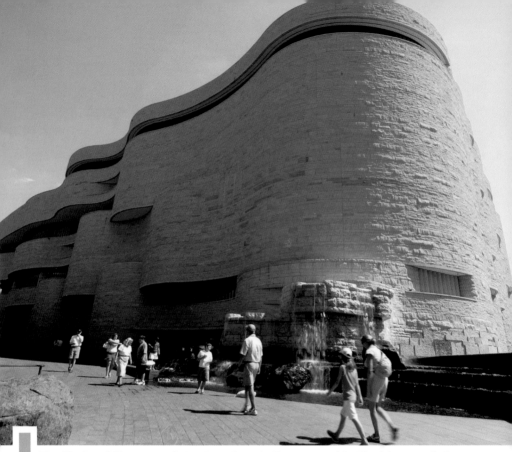

The National Museum of the American Indian opened in Washington, D.C., in 2004. It offers wide-ranging exhibits and programs to showcase the breadth of American Indian culture and history.

brand-new facilities in Washington, D.C. The five-story building holds a vast collection of American Indian artwork, artifacts, and historical records. Visitors to the museum can see authentic Native American costumes, baskets, weaving, jewelry, tools, and ritual objects. Visitors can taste traditional American Indian foods, watch Indian dancers on film, and hear Native American storytellers. Some exhibits deal with ancient history. Others concern modern Native American culture. Exhibits span thousands of years and twelve hundred different tribal groups across North, Central, and South America. Collections include historical photographs, audio recordings, films, and other media. The museum sponsors educational and outreach programs, including lectures, websites, radio shows, and traveling exhibitions.

At the ceremony dedicating the museum on September 21, 2004, museum director Richard West, a Southern Cheyenne, said, "Visitors will leave this museum knowing that Indians are not part of history. We are still here and making vital contributions to contemporary American culture and art."

▦ ▦ ▦ ▦ REVISITING THE OCCUPATION

In the late 1990s, several filmmakers, scholars, and Alcatraz veterans created a documentary film about the invasion. Called *Alcatraz Is Not an Island*, the movie features interviews with many veterans of the occupation, as well as original news footage taken in 1969 and 1970. The movie includes Richard Oakes reading the famous Indians of All Tribes proclamation. It shows LaNada Boyer and John Trudell speaking with reporters during the occupation and then, thirty years later, reflecting on their experiences on Alcatraz. The film also shows speedboats skirting around Coast Guard vessels, trying to deliver occupiers to Alcatraz, American Indian kids playing on the island, and the glorious Thanksgiving Day feast.

At the end of the movie, occupation veterans note the event's importance. "We awoke Indian people individually. We awoke tribes. We awoke the media. We awoke the United States government," said Adam Nordwall, who by then had adopted an Indian name, Adam Fortunate Eagle. "We were able to raise not only the consciousness of other American people but our own people as well," said LaNada Boyer.

"Over the years, people would come up to me and . . . I would say, I was there at the very beginning, and I was a part of that occupation, remembered Ed Castillo. "People would tell me, 'You can't imagine how that transformed my life.'" Actor Benjamin Bratt was only six years old when his mother took him and his four siblings to Alcatraz in 1970. She was a Quechua Indian, originally from Peru. Bratt grew up to become a Native American activist himself. He is the narrator of *Alcatraz Is Not an Island*.

Wilma Mankiller, the first female chief of the Cherokee Nation, visited Alcatraz several times during the occupation. She wrote in

1991, "They took over the twelve-acre [4.9-hectare] island to attract attention to the government's gross mistreatment of generations of native people. They did it to remind the whites that the land was *ours* before it was *theirs.* . . . The name of the island is Alcatraz. It changed my life forever."

Mankiller later concluded, "In a way [Alcatraz] reminds me of a flame that kind of died down but never went away. And out of that fire came all these different people, spread in all different directions to do incredible work." Grace Thorpe offered this assessment: "[The occupation] helped produce the revival of our languages. The revival of our old Indian ways, of our traditions. The Indian renaissance [rebirth]."

Wilma Mankiller spent time on Alcatraz during the occupation. She went on to become the first female chief of the Cherokee Nation and served for ten years. She died April 6, 2010.

1492: Italian navigator Christopher Columbus sails to islands in the Caribbean Sea, beginning European exploration and conquest of the Americas.

1775–1783: American colonists fight the Revolutionary War to win independence from Great Britain. Many Native American tribes fight alongside the British during the war.

1824: Congress creates the Bureau of Indian Affairs (BIA), part of the U.S. War Department, to oversee dealings with Native Americans.

1825: The U.S. government sets up Indian Country, or Indian Territory, in parts of present-day Oklahoma, Kansas, and Nebraska.

1830: Congress passes the Indian Removal Act, authorizing the relocation of Native Americans to Indian Country.

1838–1839: U.S. Army Soldiers round up about fifteen thousand Cherokee from Georgia and march them to Indian Territory. About four thousand American Indians die during this so-called Trail of Tears.

1861: A military prison opens on Alcatraz Island.

1866–1868: Sioux and Cheyenne warriors fight against U.S. troops in Red Cloud's War in Montana.

1868: The U.S. government and the Sioux sign the Treaty of Fort Laramie, or Sioux Treaty of 1868, ending Red Cloud's War.

1876: Sioux, Cheyenne, and Arapaho warriors defeat a cavalry unit led by U.S. general George Custer on the banks of the Little Bighorn River in Montana.

1879: U.S. Army officer Richard H. Pratt founds the first government-funded American Indian school in Carlisle, Pennsylvania.

1887: Congress passes the Dawes Act. This law breaks up American Indian lands into small parcels and gives parcels to Indian families and individuals, who are then directed to farm the land.

1890: U.S. troops kill more than two hundred Sioux men, women, and children at Wounded Knee Creek in South Dakota.

1924: Congress passes the Indian Citizenship Act, granting full citizenship rights to Native Americans.

1928: The Meriam Report describes the poverty and bleak conditions on U.S. Indian reservations.

1934: Congress passes the Indian Reorganization Act, part of the New Deal, to improve life for Native Americans. Alcatraz Island becomes the site of a federal penitentiary (prison).

1946: Congress creates the Indian Claims Commission (ICC) to settle historic disputes over broken treaties.

1952: Congress creates a voluntary relocation program to move American Indians from reservations to big U.S. cities.

1953: The U.S. government begins the termination program, ending BIA protections for certain American Indian tribes.

1957–1975: The United States fights the Vietnam War.

1959: The ICC compensates California Indians for stolen lands at the rate of 47 cents per acre (19 cents per hectare), a payment based on 1853 land values.

1961: Young Native Americans form the National Indian Youth Council (NIYC). The NIYC stages "fish-ins" in Washington State. Adam Nordwall and others form the United Bay Area Council, an umbrella group for Indian organizations in the San Francisco–Oakland area.

1963: The U.S. government closes the federal prison on Alcatraz.

1964: Members of the San Francisco Sioux Club and other Amercian Indians stage a symbolic invasion of Alcatraz Island on March 8.

1968: LaNada Boyer and Lehman Brightman form United Native Americans at UC–Berkeley. Students at San Francisco State College go on strike to demand higher minority enrollment and ethnic studies programs. Activists in Minneapolis, Minnesota, form the American Indian Movement (AIM).

1969: From January to March, UC–Berkeley students stage a Third World Strike to demand ethnic studies programs. In October the San Francisco American Indian Center burns down. On November 9, Indians gather at Pier 39 in San Francisco to begin an invasion of Alcatraz, but the boats do not arrive. Richard

Oakes reads the Indians of All Tribes proclamation on the pier. The *Monte Cristo* takes fifty passengers to circle Alcatraz. Five American Indians jump off the boat and swim to Alcatraz. The *New Vera II* returns with another group that night, and fourteen Indians spend the night on Alcatraz. On November 20, ninety-two American Indians land on Alcatraz and set up a permanent occupation. On November 27, occupiers celebrate Thanksgiving on Alcatraz, with food provided by a restaurant in San Francisco.

1970: On January 3, twelve-year-old Yvonne Oakes falls off a third-floor-landing balcony on Alcatraz and dies four days later. In February, mainland Indian leaders form the Bay Area Native American Council to negotiate with the U.S. government. In May the government hauls away the water barge and shuts off electricity and phone service on Alcatraz. Occupiers celebrate Indian Liberation Day and draft the Declaration of the Return of Indian Land. In June, fires burn the warden's house, lighthouse, and several other structures on Alcatraz. On July 8, President Richard Nixon delivers a speech on Indian policy to Congress. He announces an end to termination, the return of sacred Blue Lake to the Indian people of Taos Pueblo, and other gains for Native Americans. In November, American Indians commemorate the first anniversary of the Alcatraz occupation on both the mainland and the island. AIM symbolically captures the *Mayflower II* in Plymouth, Massachusetts, on Thanksgiving Day.

1971: The federal government removes the remaining fifteen occupiers from Alcatraz in early June.

1972: The National Park Service takes over Alcatraz. A security guard kills Richard Oakes at a YMCA camp in northern California.

Members of AIM and the NIYC drive to Washington, D.C., for the Trail of Broken Treaties protest. The group takes over the BIA headquarters for one week.

1973: The former prison on Alcatraz opens to tourists. AIM fighters occupy Wounded Knee on the Pine Ridge Reservation in South Dakota and hold off federal agents for seventy-one days.

1975: AIM fighters kill two federal agents on the Pine Ridge Reservation.

1978: American Indians march cross-country from Sacramento, California, to Washington, D.C., on the Longest Walk to protest anti-Indian legislation introduced in Congress.

1992: American Indians protest the Columbus quincentenary (five-hundredth anniversary of landing) with various actions across the United States.

2004: The National Museum of the American Indian opens in a new facility in Washington, D.C.

2009: At the annual "Un-Thanksgiving" celebration on Alcatraz Island, American Indians mark the fortieth anniversary of the occupation of the island.

2010: Occupation leader Adam Fortunate Eagle is the subject of a documentary film, *Contrary Warrior: The Life and Times of Adam Fortunate Eagle*.

Peter Blue Cloud

(b. 1935) A Mohawk, Blue Cloud was born on the Caughnawaga Reserve (the Canadian equivalent of a reservation) in Kahnawake, Quebec, Canada. As a young man, he held various jobs, as a logger, a carpenter, and an ironworker. In the 1960s, he became involved in American Indian activism and was part of the November 20, 1969, Alcatraz invasion. On Alcatraz he published the *Indians of All Tribes Newsletter* in the early months of the occupation. In 1972 Blue Cloud wrote a memoir, *Alcatraz Is Not an Island*, about his experiences with the occupation. He also wrote for *Indian Magazine* and for *Akwesasne Notes*, a national Indian newspaper. Blue Cloud has published many books of poetry and short stories. Many of his works combine Native American myths and legends with examinations of issues facing modern-day Native Americans.

LaNada Boyer

(b. 1947) Boyer was born in Blackfoot, Idaho, on the Bannock-Shoshone Fort Hall Reservation. When she was a child, her father was the tribal chairman. Boyer attended several Indian schools, where teachers sometimes made demeaning comments about Native Americans. These comments and other injustices made her angry and rebellious. Several times, she was expelled from school. In 1965 she volunteered for the relocation program and moved to San Francisco. In 1968 Boyer entered UC–Berkeley on a scholarship for minority students. At first she was one of just two American Indians on campus. The university soon admitted additional Indian students, and Boyer became a leader of this group. She founded the radical student group United Native Americans and took part in the 1969 Third World Strike at Berkeley. With thirteen others, Boyer spent the night on Alcatraz on November 9, 1969, and returned on November 20 with the permanent occupation. During the occupation, she commuted to the mainland to continue her studies at Berkeley. She and John Trudell took the reins of leadership during the final year of the occupation. After the occupation ended, Boyer returned to the Fort Hall Reservation in Idaho. She went on to earn a PhD in political science.

Ed Castillo

(b. 1949) A member of the Cahuilla and Luiseño tribes of California, Castillo was the first one in his family to attend college. At the University of California–Riverside, he was one of only three minority students in an undergraduate population of about three thousand. After graduating in 1969, Castillo took a job teaching American Indian history at the University of California–Los Angeles, which had only recently admitted its first Indian students. Castillo joined these students for the November 20, 1969, occupation of Alcatraz. He was elected to the first All Tribes Council and put in charge of island security. Castillo remained on Alcatraz for more than three months and then returned to his teaching job at UCLA. The following year, he began graduate studies in the History Department at UC–Berkeley. In the late 1980s, Castillo joined the faculty of Sonoma State University in Rohnert Park, California. He heads the university's Native American Studies Department and has written several books on the history of California Indians.

Adam (Nordwall) Fortunate Eagle

(b. 1929) A Chippewa (or Ojibwa), Nordwall was born on the Red Lake Reservation in northern Minnesota. When he was five, the Bureau of Indian Affairs sent him to the Pipestone Indian Training School in southwestern Minnesota. After graduation from Pipestone, Nordwall moved on to Haskell Institute in Kansas, a combination Indian high school and junior college. At Haskell, Nordwall studied commercial art. He married and moved to San Francisco, where his mother was then living. He took a job with a pest extermination company and then moved with his family to suburban San Leandro, where he opened his own extermination business. He and others founded the United Bay Area Council in 1961, and Nordwall became chairman of the organization. He took part in the 1964 invasion of Alcatraz and was among the main organizers of the November 9, 1969, invasion. He visited Alcatraz several times during the occupation but never lived there. He was part of BANAC, the mainland group that negotiated with the federal government during the occupation. After the occupation, Nordwall took the name Adam Fortunate Eagle, a name given to him by leaders of the Crow Nation in Montana. In 1976 he and his family left San Leandro and moved to the Shoshone reservation in Nevada, his wife's birthplace. Nordwall has written several books on the Alcatraz occupation.

Earl Livermore

(b. 1932) Livermore was born on the Blackfoot Reservation in northwestern Montana. He attended college at the University of Washington in Seattle and the Academy of Art in San Francisco. While creating his own paintings, prints, and pottery, he also worked as executive director of the San Francisco American Indian Center, a key gathering spot for American Indians in the Bay Area in the 1960s. After the Alcatraz invasion, Livermore quit his job and set up an Indian arts and crafts center on Alcatraz. There, he and other Indian artists gave lessons in traditional Indian beadwork, leatherwork, wood carving, and sculpture.

After the occupation, Livermore earned a master's degree in education from Harvard University. He also continued to make and sell his own artwork. His work has been exhibited at both Indian and non-Indian art galleries and museums. Many of his works include traditional Native American motifs.

Wilma Mankiller

(1945–2010) Mankiller was born on the Cherokee Reservation in Tahlequah, Oklahoma. Her family moved to the San Francisco area when the U.S. Army took over their land to expand a military base. Mankiller married an Ecuadorian student in 1963, and had two daughters. She became active in the San Francisco Indian Center and the occupation of Alcatraz. Divorced, Mankiller moved with her daughters back to Oklahoma in 1977. She began working for the Cherokee Nation, one of the largest tribes in the United States. In 1983 she was elected deputy chief (similar to vice president) of the Cherokee Nation. When the chief resigned, she inherited the office. Despite opposition from some Cherokee people who did not want a female leader, she ran for chief in 1987 and won. As chief she organized many community development projects, established Cherokee-owned businesses, and improved daily life by providing running water and electricity to poor families. Because of health concerns, Mankiller decided not to run for chief in 1995. She wrote a book and taught courses on Indian law and government at several U.S. universities. She died in Oklahoma in 2010.

Russell Means

(b.1939) Means was born on the Pine Ridge Indian Reservation in South Dakota and moved with his family to the San Francisco area when he was a child. As a young man, he became involved in the fight for Indian rights. He moved to Cleveland, Ohio, where he served as director of that city's American Indian Center. Means met Dennis Banks, cofounder of American Indian Movement, in 1968. In 1969 he took part in the Indian occupation of Alcatraz. He became the first national director of AIM in 1970. Under his direction, AIM protested at Mount Rushmore in South Dakota and seized the *Mayflower II* in Plymouth, Massachusetts, to spotlight American Indian causes. In 1973 Means led AIM's occupation of Wounded Knee, which ended in armed confrontation with the FBI. In 1992 Means took up acting. He played Indian characters on TV and in movies. He played Chief Chingachgook in the film *The Last of the Mohicans* (1992) and was the voice of Pocahontas's father in the animated film *Pocahontas* (1995). Means remains involved in both acting and the Native American rights movement.

Dorothy Lonewolf Miller

(1920–2003) Part Blackfoot, Miller was born in West Liberty, Iowa. She worked as a union organizer in the 1940s, a job that set her on an activist path. In 1955 she earned a master's degree in social work from the University of Iowa. She earned a PhD in social welfare from UC–Berkeley in 1967. While studying at Berkeley, Miller founded the Scientific Analysis Corporation. This nonprofit firm carried out research on mental health, prison reform, alcoholism, runaway youths, and urban American Indians. During the Alcatraz occupation, Miller set up the Indians of All Tribes bank account and set up radio communications between the island and the mainland. She served as executive director of the Scientific Analysis Corporation until her retirement in 2000.

Richard Oakes

(1942–1972) Oakes was born on the St. Regis Mohawk Reservation in upstate New York, near the border with Canada. Not much is known about his early life. According to rumors, as a young man, Oakes worked high in the air, building skyscrapers in New York City—a job held by many Mohawk men in the early and mid twentieth century. Many people doubt this story. Oakes made his way to San Francisco around 1968. He enrolled in San Francisco State College, where he took part in the Third World Strike of 1968–1969. He was among the main organizers of the Alcatraz invasion and quickly became the unofficial spokesperson for the occupation. Oakes and his family left Alcatraz after the death of his daughter Yvonne in early 1970. He took part in a number of other Native American protests in the following year and a half. In the fall of 1972, a security guard at a YMCA camp in northern California shot Oakes during a dispute. The killing angered the American Indian activist community and in part inspired the Trail of Broken Treaties protest and BIA occupation later that fall. In 1999 Oakes's former college, by then known as San Francisco State University, opened the Richard Oakes Multicultural Center in his honor.

Grace Thorpe

(1921–2008) Grace Thorpe was born in Yale, Oklahoma. Her father was the legendary athlete Jim Thorpe. A member of the Sac and Fox tribe, Grace Thorpe joined the Women's Army Corps (WAC) during World War II (1939–1945). The WAC sent her to New Guinea, the Philippines, and Japan, where she worked for famous U.S. general Douglas MacArthur. She earned a Bronze Star medal for her wartime achievements. After the war, Thorpe earned a bachelor's degree from the University of Tennessee and a paralegal degree from the Antioch School of Law in Washington, D.C. During her long career, Thorpe worked for American Indian rights. She worked for the U.S. Senate Indian Affairs Committee, the National Congress of American Indians, the National Environmental Coalition of Native Americans, and other organizations. She also worked as a tribal judge and a health commissioner for the Sac and Fox tribe in Oklahoma. When Indian students took over Alcatraz in 1969, Thorpe quit her job, put her furniture in storage, and spent her life savings to join the occupation. She handled much of the media relations in the early months of the occupation. She eventually left to take part in American Indian activist projects elsewhere. Her daughter, Dagmar, also took part in the occupation.

John Trudell

(b. 1946) A Santee Sioux, Trudell was born in Omaha, Nebraska. As a child, he divided his time between Omaha and the Santee Sioux Reservation in northern Nebraska. At seventeen Trudell joined the U.S. Navy. After his service, he moved to California. He enrolled in UCLA to study radio and television broadcasting. He came to Alcatraz for the 1969 Thanksgiving celebration. He was so inspired by this visit that he moved with his wife and children to Alcatraz. He began broadcasting the weekly *Radio Free Alcatraz* program and eventually became a leader of the occupation. After the occupation ended, Trudell served as chairman of AIM for six years. In the 1980s, Trudell turned his energy to the arts. He wrote poetry, recorded music, and acted in films and television. He remains involved in American Indian activism and other political causes.

BIA: The Bureau of Indian Affairs is part of the U.S. Department of the Interior. It is responsible for managing Indian land held in trust by the U.S. government. It was the group in charge of sending Indian children to boarding schools. The BIA also acted to prevent Native American uprisings and protests.

colonize: to take over a territory by creating settlements there

hunter-gatherers: people who get food by hunting wild animals and gathering wild plants. Many Indians of North America were hunter-gatherers prior to the European conquest.

Indian boarding schools: nineteenth- and twentieth-century schools for American Indian children run by the U.S. government, churches, and private organizations. The schools took Indian children away from their families and taught them —often by force— to adopt the customs of mainstream white society.

mission: a building complex for religious groups who teach religious doctrine to those in the surrounding area. During the years of European exploration and colonization of the Americas, many European church groups set up missions in Indian lands, mostly in the western United States.

powwow: an Indian meeting or social gathering

relocation: the movement of people from one community to another. In the nineteenth century, the U.S. government forced many American Indians to relocate to Indian Territory and to reservations. In the twentieth century, the government asked American Indians to voluntarily relocate from reservations to cities.

reservation: a parcel of land set aside by the U.S. government as a home for Native Americans

termination: an ending. The Indian termination program of the twentieth century ended the special relationship between certain tribes and the U.S. government. Tribes that were terminated lost all Bureau of Indian Affairs protection and assistance.

treaty: an agreement in writing between two nations or groups

ward: a person under the protection and care of the government. American Indians were wards of the U.S. government until the Indian Citizenship Act of 1924. Some aspects of Indian wardship continued after this date.

5 Troy R. Johnson, *The American Indian Occupation of Alcatraz Island: Red Power and Self-Determination* (Lincoln: University of Nebraska Press, 1996), 114.

6 *Alcatraz Is Not an Island*, DVD, directed by James M. Fortier (Berkeley, CA: Diamond Island Productions, 2001).

7 Johnson, *American Indian Occupation*, 67.

7 *Alcatraz Is Not an Island.*

8 James Wilson, *The Earth Shall Weep: A History of Native America* (New York: Atlantic Monthly Press, 1998), 219.

15 Robert F. Berkhofer Jr., *The White Man's Indian: Images of the American Indian from Columbus to the Present* (New York: Vintage Books, 1979), 21.

22 Peter Nabokov, ed., *Native American Testimony: A Chronicle of Indian-White Relations from Prophecy to the Present, 1492–1992* (New York: Viking, 1991), 165.

24 Dee Brown, *Bury My Heart at Wounded Knee: An Indian History of the American West* (New York: Henry Holt and Company, 1970), 169.

28 Ibid., 170.

30 Nabokov, *Native American Testimony*, 179.

30–31 Wilson, *Earth Shall Weep*, 243.

31 Brown, *Bury My Heart at Wounded Knee*, 446.

32 Charla Bear, "American Indian Boarding Schools Haunt Many," National Public Radio, May 12, 2008, http://www.npr.org/templates/story/story.php?storyid=16516865 (January 27, 2010).

33–34 Nabokov, *Native American Testimony*, 182.

34 Berkhofer, *White Man's Indian*, 173.

34 Bear, "American Indian Boarding Schools."

34 Ibid.

44 Jeannette Henry, *Textbooks and the American Indian* (San Francisco: Indian Historian Press, 1970), 37.

44 Ibid., 40.

44 Ibid., 59.

45 Bear, "American Indian Boarding Schools."

46 Johnson, *American Indian Occupation*, 101.

51 Johnson, Champagne, and Nagel, "American Indian Activism and Transformation," in Johnson, Nagel, and Champagne, *American Indian Activism*, 9–44.

53 Adam Fortunate Eagle, *Heart of the Rock: The Indian Invasion of Alcatraz*, with Tim Findley (Norman: University of Oklahoma Press, 2002), 37.

55 Ibid., 9.

55 Johnson, *American Indian Occupation*, 17.

57 Ibid., 16.

57 Ibid.

59 Henry, *Textbooks*, 41.

60 Johnson, Champagne, and Nagel, "American Indian Activism and Transformation," in Johnson, Nagel, and Champagne, *American Indian Activism*, 9–44.

61 Troy Johnson, Duane Champagne, and Joane Nagel, "American Indian Activism and Transformation: Lessons from Alcatraz," in *American Indian Activism: Alcatraz to the Longest Walk*, eds. Troy Johnson, Joane Nagel, and Duane Champagne, 9–44 (Urbana: University of Illinois Press, 1997).

62   San Francisco State Magazine, "Remember the Strike," Fall–Winter 2008, http://www.sfsu.edu/~sfsumag/archive/fall_08/strike.html (January 27, 2010).

66   Johnson, American Indian Occupation, 54-55.

69–70   Johnson, American Indian Occupation, 53–54.

70   Ibid., 54–55.

71   Johnson, American Indian Occupation, 63.

72   Adam (Nordwall) Fortunate Eagle, "Urban Indians and the Occupation of Alcatraz Island," in Johnson, Nagel, and Champagne, American Indian Activism, 52–73.

73   Johnson, American Indian Occupation, 63.

73   Fortunate Eagle, "Urban Indians and the Occupation of Alcatraz," in Johnson, Nagel, and Champagne, American Indian Activism, 52–73.

75   Fortunate Eagle, Heart of the Rock, 106.

75   Ibid., 107.

76   Ibid., 115.

78   Johnson, American Indian Occupation, 97.

85   Robert A. Runstrom, "American Indian Placemaking on Alcatraz, 1969–71," in Johnson, Nagel, and Champagne, American Indian Activism, 186–206.

87   Fortunate Eagle, Heart of the Rock, 92.

89   Robert A. Runstrom, "American Indian Placemaking on Alcatraz, 1969–71," in Johnson, Nagel, and Champagne, American Indian Activism, 186–206.

90   Alcatraz Is Not an Island.

90   George Horse Capture, "From the Reservation to the Smithsonian via Alcatraz," in Johnson, Nagel, and Champagne, American Indian Activism, 140–152.

90   Alcatraz Is Not an Island.

91   Tim Findley, "Alcatraz Recollections," in Johnson, Nagel, and Champagne, American Indian Activism, 74–87.

92   Johnson, American Indian Occupation, 173.

94   Ibid., 81–82.

95   Fortunate Eagle, Heart of the Rock, 162.

97   Alcatraz Is Not an Island.

99   Johnson, American Indian Occupation, 187.

100   Alcatraz Is Not an Island.

100   Johnson, American Indian Occupation, 192.

101   Ibid., 129.

102   Richard Nixon, "Special Message to the Congress on Indian Affairs, July 8, 1970" American Presidency Project, 2010, http://www.presidency.ucsb.edu/ws/index.php?pid=2573 (January 27, 2010).

103   John Garvey and Troy Johnson, "The Government and the Indians: The American Indian Occupation of Alcatraz Island, 1969–71," in Johnson, Nagel, and Champagne, American Indian Activism, 153–185.

104   Fortunate Eagle, Heart of the Rock, 182.

108   Richard Nixon, "Special Message to the Congress on Indian Affairs, July 8, 1970," American Presidency Project, 2010, http://www.presidency.ucsb.edu/ws/index.php?pid=2573 (January 27, 2010).

116 *Alcatraz Is Not an Island.*

117 *Time,* "Anomie at Alcatraz," April
     12, 1971, http://www
     .time.com/time/magazine/
     article/0,9171,904960,00.html
     (January 27, 2010).

117 Garvey and Johnson,
     "Government and the Indians,"
     in Johnson, Nagel, and
     Champagne, *Native American
     Activism,* 153–185.

117 Johnson, *American Indian Occupation,*
     210.

117–118 Findley, "Alcatraz
     Recollections," in Johnson,
     Nagel, and Champagne, *Native
     American Activism,* 74–87.

118 Fortunate Eagle, *Heart of the Rock,*
     198.

119 Garvey and Johnson,
     "Government and the Indians, in
     Johnson, Nagel, and Champagne,
     Native American Activism, 153–185.

122 Ward Churchill, "The Bloody
     Wake of Alcatraz: Political
     Repression of the American
     Indian Movement during the
     1970s," in Johnson, Nagel,
     and Champagne, *Native American
     Activism,* 242–284.

129 Lee Ranck, "To Save Their Indian
     Way of Life," 1978, Longest
     Walk, 2008. http://longestwalk.
     org/index.php?option=com_co
     ntent&task=blogcategory&id=
     33&Itemid=108 (January 27,
     2010).

130 Liska Koenig, "Occupation of
     Alcatraz Island Remembered,"
     December 2009, *Guardsman,*
     http://theguardsman.
     com/2009/12/(January 27,
     2010).

134 Ibid.

136 Ian S. McIntosh, "A Museum for
     the Americas," *Cultural Survival
     Quarterly,* Winter 2004, 2009,
     http://www
     .culturalsurvival.org/
     publications/cultural-survival-
     quarterly/ian-s-mcintosh/
     museum-americas (January 27,
     2010).

136 *Alcatraz Is Not an Island.*

137 Johnson, *American Indian Occupation,*
     129.

137 *Alcatraz Is Not an Island.*

137 Ibid.

Alcatraz Is Not an Island. DVD. Directed by James M. Fortier. Berkeley, CA: Diamond Island Productions, 2001.

Berkhofer, Robert F., Jr. *The White Man's Indian: Images of the American Indian from Columbus to the Present*. New York: Vintage Books, 1979.

Brown, Dee. *Bury My Heart at Wounded Knee: An Indian History of the American West*. New York: Henry Holt and Company, 1970.

Cameron, Robert. *Alcatraz: A Visual Essay*. San Francisco: Cameron and Company, 1989.

Deloria, Vine, Jr. *Custer Died for Your Sins: An Indian Manifesto*. Norman: University of Oklahoma Press, 1969.

Fortunate Eagle, Adam. *Heart of the Rock: The Indian Invasion of Alcatraz*. With Tim Findley. Norman: University of Oklahoma Press, 2002.

Henry, Jeannette. *Textbooks and the American Indian*. San Francisco: Indian Historian Press, 1970.

Johnson, Troy R. *The American Indian Occupation of Alcatraz: Red Power and Self-Determination*. Lincoln: University of Nebraska Press, 1996.

Johnson, Troy, Joane Nagel, and Duane Champagne, eds. *American Indian Activism: Alcatraz to the Longest Walk*. Urbana: University of Illinois Press, 1997.

Margolin, Malcolm. *The Ohlone Way: Indian Life in the San Francisco–Monterey Bay Area*. Berkeley, CA: Heyday Books, 1978.

Nabokov, Peter, ed. *Native American Testimony: A Chronicle of Indian-White Relations from Prophecy to the Present, 1492–1992*. New York: Viking, 1991.

Waldman, Carl. *Atlas of the North American Indian*. 3rd ed. New York: Checkmark Books, 2009.

Wilson, James. *The Earth Shall Weep: A History of Native America*. New York: Atlantic Monthly Press, 1998.

Books

Behrman, Carol. *The Indian Wars*. Minneapolis: Twenty-First Century Books, 2004. In a series of conflicts called the Indian Wars, white Europeans nearly destroyed Native American people and culture. This book chronicles those wars, with detailed information about soldiers, military leaders, weapons, and battles.

Dunn, John M. *The Relocation of the North American Indian*. Farmington Hills, MI: Lucent Books, 2005. As Europeans explored and settled North America, they simultaneously declared war on the American Indian. Over several centuries of conflict, millions of American Indians lost their lives. Most of the survivors ended up confined to reservations. This book tells the tragic story.

Lindop, Edmund. *America in the 1960s*. Minneapolis: Twenty-First Century Books, 2010. The Alcatraz occupation began during the tumultuous 1960s, a decade of protest and social upheaval. This book explores the civil rights movement, the antiwar movement, and other social protests that inspired the red power movement of the late 1960s and early 1970s.

Murdoc, David S. *North American Indian*. New York: DK Children, 2005. This exquisitely designed title provides a comprehensive look at Indian cultures across North America. Readers will learn about American Indian history and lifeways, as well as modern-day American Indian society. Photographs, maps, and illustrations enhance the text.

Sonneborn, Liz. *The American Indian Experience*. Minneapolis: Twenty-First Century Books, 2010. Part of the Cultural Mosaic series, this title explores the contributions of American Indians to U.S. literature, arts, entertainment, and sports. The book also examines Native American religious traditions, festivals, and cooking.

Websites

Alcatraz: Taking Back "The Rock"
http://www.nativepeoples.com/article/articles/144/1/Alcatraz-Taking-Back-quotThe-Rockquot/Page1.html
This Web page offers a lengthy article about the occupation from *Native Peoples* magazine. The piece includes photographs and interviews with occupiers LaNada Boyer, John Trudell, and others.

Alcatraz Is Not an Island
http://www.pbs.org/itvs/alcatrazisnotanisland/index.html
The website is a companion to the documentary film of the same name. Visitors will learn about the history of American Indian activism, the Alcatraz occupation, and the people who made it happen.

American Indian Movement (AIM)
http://www.aimovement.org
This AIM website gives a history of the movement and information on the many areas in which AIM continues to fight for Native American rights. There is also a link to AIM webcasts and AIM radio broadcasts.

PHOTO ACKNOWLEDGMENTS

The images in this book are used with the permission of:
SAN FRANCISCO HISTORY CENTER, SAN FRANCISCO PUBLIC LIBRARY, pp. 5, 115;
AP Photo, pp. 7, 54, 82, 83, 109; © Georg Heinrich/CORBIS, p. 10; © Marilyn Angel
Wynn/Nativestock.com, p. 12; © MPI/Getty Images, pp. 14, 16, 26, 105;
© W. Langdon Kihn/National Geographic/CORBIS, p. 20; © Bettmann/CORBIS, pp.
23, 35 56, 62, 64-65, 75, 84, 93, 122, 125, 126; © Transcendental Graphics/Getty
Images, p. 25; © Roger-Violet/The Image Works, p. 28; Library of Congress (LC-
USZ61-2085), p. 30, (LC-USZ62-26792), p. 36; © akg-images/The Image Works, p.
38; © USMC/Hulton Archive/Getty Images, p. 43; © Argosy Pictures Corporation/
Ronald Grant Archive/Mary Evans/The Image Works, p. 44; © 2011 Ilka Hartmann,
pp. 47, 48, 80, 103, 131, 133; © Matt Heron/Take Stock/The Image Works, p. 49;
Courtesy, Adam Fortunate Eagle Nordwall, p. 53; © Jason Laure/The Image Works,
p. 58; © Laura Westlund/Independent Picture Service, pp. 68, 132; AP Photo/Robert
W. Klein, p. 72; © UPI TELEPHOTO/CORBIS, pp. 74, 79; © William James Warren/
CORBIS, p. 77; © Brooks Townes, pp. 81, 86; AP Photo/ Walter Zeboski, p. 88;
© Vince Maggiora/San Francisco Chronicle, pp. 96, 118; Courtesy of The Bancroft
Library, University of California, Berkeley (BANC PIC 2003.108--NEG, box 22.1990B.
FR 6A)/© Michelle Vignes, p. 97; © CORBIS, p. 104; © RB/Redferns/Getty Images,
p. 106; © Fox Photos/Getty Images, p. 107; Courtesy of The Bancroft Library,
University of California, Berkeley, (BANC PIC 2003.108, box > 22.1990:1A--NEG.)/
© Michelle Vignes, p. 112; © Michael Springer/Getty Images, p. 113; AP Photo/Sal
Veder, p. 119; AP Photo/Robert W. Klein, p. 120; AP Photo/Paul C. Strong, p. 128;
© Mark Wilson/Getty Images, p. 135; Diana Walker/Getty Images, p. 137.

Front cover: © 2011 Ilka Hartmann.

ABOUT THE AUTHOR

Margaret J. Goldstein was born in Detroit, Michigan, and graduated from the University
of Michigan. She is an editor and author of books for young readers. She lives in
northern New Mexico.